A New Introduction to the Spiritual Exercises of St. Ignatius

Henry F. Birkenhauer, S.J.
Tad Dunne
Walter L. Farrell, S.J.
Howard J. Gray, S.J.
Kenneth J. Galbraith, S.J.
Jules Toner, S.J.
Peter J. Fennessy, S.J.
Shannon Barnes
John A. McGrail, S.J.
John E. Dister, S.J.

John E. Dister, S.J., Editor

Foreword by Walter J. Burghardt, S.J.

Wipf and Stock Publishers
EUGENE, OREGON

Wipf and Stock Publishers
199 West 8th Avenue, Suite 3
Eugene, Oregon 97401

A New Introduction to the Exercises of St. Ignatius
Edited by Dister, John E.
Copyright© January, 1993 Dister, John E.
ISBN: 1-59244-274-9
Print Date: June, 2003
Previously published by Liturgical Press, January, 1993 .

Contents

Foreword

Recent proponents of a philosophical hermeneutics insist that the genius of a "classic"—Sophocles or Shakespeare, Scripture or Chopin—is that the masterpiece in question invariably contains more than the original artist(s) could have consciously known or explicitly intended. In consequence, the classical text is never exhausted by the commentary of an individual or the interpretation of an age. There is always room for further discovery, for fresh insights, for contemporary applications. And this not by going beyond the text; what is newly presented stems from the text itself. This is not a reading *into* the text; it is a reading *out of* the text.

Such, I suggest, is a fascinating facet of Ignatius Loyola's *Spiritual Exercises*. (The suggestion is my own, not to be foisted on Father Dister and his collaborators.) After four and a half centuries, we are not only continuing to grasp what was Ignatius' explicit intent in the course of the Four Weeks; we are unearthing ideas and insights that, perhaps paradoxically, were not in the pilgrim saint's mind but are germinally in his text. When I compare the *Exercises* as commented and preached today with the *Exercises* presented to me in my noviceship (1931–33) and tertianship (1942–43), I am amazed, in awe, delighted. This slender book ceaselessly opens up like a flower, especially in the hands of knowledgeable, imaginative interpreters.

Such are the interpreters who have shaped the volume at hand. Some examples. Take the First Week. On the one hand, the authors insist on what should have been clear from the beginning: For Ignatius, Christ is central to the very first Week of the *Exercises*, critical to the process of conversion, of reform. On the other hand, we learn what is not explicit in the text but is a legitimate understanding in the context of our culture: The reform to which the Ignatian retreat looks is not a Lone Ranger or Don Quixote *sola fide* effort but a collaborative enterprise of corporate conversion where faith expresses itself in work for justice, and justice requires political science, psychology, and economics.

Take the Second Week. On the one hand, the "Call of the King" explicitly envisions a lord/vassal relationship, though in a form of service that demands mutual fidelity. On the other hand, the ideal king may be imagined as any leader who can win hearts and inspire devotion. In fact, the king can legitimately be seen as my transcendent self, the living principle of generativity, fertility, and creativity. And Christ is not simply male but the androgynous male, humanity male and female, ceaselessly moving to wholeness and unity-in-difference.

Ignatius' "discernment of spirits" is found to be useful not only for those who, like Ignatius, believe in angels and demons, but also for those in our culture who do not interpret these biblical images literally but limit "spirits" to the tendencies in our own psyches that spring from egotism and disordered sensuality, from other humans, and from our society.

Take the Third Week. On the one hand, in its theology of dying with Christ in order to enter into his life, it is hardly uniquely Ignatian, is not particularly unusual among Christian spiritualities. On the other hand, what one of this volume's interpreters draws somewhat subtly from Ignatius is the importance of the contemplation on the burial of Christ—a contemplation that "brings us out of suffering and pain into a stillness where there is no longer any desire or fear, no rejoicing over good, no sorrow over pain." This "utter stillness and motionlessness of death," this silence, is the goal of the Week, the perfection of Ignatian indifference. Out of this silence will come an experience of the risen Christ.

Take the Fourth Week. On the one hand, Ignatius did see Jesus' resurrection (with the Contemplation for Learning To Love Like God) as the climax of the *Exercises,* as not simply glorious history but ongoing redemption, Christ alive now, our joy in the risen Lord. On the other hand, he could hardly have foreseen the impact on his *Exercises* of a fresh theological understanding of the resurrection, such as was initiated by scholars like F. X. Durrwell, David Stanley, and Gerald Collins. But the *Exercises* are wondrously open to all this.

There is more, far more. On the one hand, we are aware that Ignatius directed many lay people in the *Exercises* long before his ordination, with a spirituality not at all monastic but focused on the "contemplative in action." On the other hand, Ignatius could hardly have conceived of a Catholic laity as numerous and culturally diverse as that of the late twentieth century, where scientific sophistication coexists with woeful ignorance, "overpopulation" with perhaps 50 million abortions a year; where the call for unprecedented freedom clashes with institutionalized serfdom, feminism with traditional roles for women; where Ignatius' Rules for Thinking with the Church must do mortal battle with an aggressive confrontation with hierarchical authority; where insistence on a faith that does justice seems hypocritical to whose who organize for rights *within* the Church. The demand for a profound and practical lay spirituality challenges the Ignatian director today as rarely in the past.

Finally, two principles fundamental to Christian spirituality are seen to emerge from Ignatius himself: (1) Karl Rahner has suggested that Ignatius' most significant contribution to the Church is his insistence that the Christian can experience God in some genuinely direct fashion, that this is a grace not simply reserved for an elite but offered to the average Christian. (2) The risen Christ is ceaselessly at work ("like a laborer") in every nook and corner, every created reality, in his universe. What our age and cultures must do is to tease out the theological and spiritual insights that such breath-taking principles imply, e.g., for a spirituality of "contemplation in action" and for a profound awareness that co-laboring with Christ is always a social, communal affair whose locale is the Church and the human family.

For me, in reading these chapters I have time and again been surprised by the joy of discovery; for I have been privileged (1) to realize afresh how pertinent Ignatius' *Spiritual Exercises* are for each new age, and (2) to grasp, for the first time, how each age and culture can legitimately discover in this slender "classic" meanings, insights, and interpretations that pass beyond the explicit intent of Ignatius and yet do not betray his thought at all.

Walter J. Burghardt, S.J.
Preaching the Just Word
Washington, D.C.
July 31, 1993

Preface

This book results from a public lecture series that was held at John Carroll University in the fall semester of 1987 in conjunction with a course on the *Spiritual Exercises* of St. Ignatius. The attendance at the eleven lectures in the series ranged consistently between 150 and 250 on a Monday evening. At least half of those in attendance were lay people. These facts are some indication that the *Spiritual Exercises* are an important topic in renewal that is taking place in American Catholicism. As the series progressed, many of those in attendance strongly urged the publication of the lectures. Not all of the lectures, however, lent themselves to editing for publication and one of the lecturers demurred on publication. I coordinated the series and introduced the speakers, but I did not contribute a lecture to that series. The final chapter is my effort to provide a unified conclusion to a series of presentations that, although surely reflecting creatively on a single and important topic, at the outset were not intended to issue in a unified book. Besides editing the lectures, with a few exceptions quite lightly, and the just mentioned added final chapter, I have added italicized introductory paragraphs to each of the chapters for that same objective of clarification and unity. The order of the chapters of this collection does not always correspond with that of the original lecture series for reasons that should be obvious in the unfolding of the chapters.

The lecturers in the series came from a variety of backgrounds and experience with the *Spiritual Exercises*. Henry F. Birkenhauer is currently superior of the Jesuit community in Columbus, Ohio, and a spiritual director at St. Theresa's Retreat House there. His career includes many years of teaching mathematics and as director of the seismology observatory at John Carroll University in Cleveland. He was later director of tertians for the Jesuit Detroit Province for five years. He returned to John Carroll as assistant to the president for two years and then was himself president there from 1970–1980. Subsequently he was vicar for religious for the diocese of Cleveland and rector of St. John's High School, Toledo, Ohio.

Through these many years he has been a much sought after retreat director and spiritual guide.

Tad Dunne has his doctorate from St. Michael's College in Toronto. He taught theology there from 1975–1983. He has published *We Cannot Find Word* (Dimension, 1981), *Lonergan and Spirituality* (Loyola University Press, 1985), *The Spiritual Exercises Today* (Harper Collins, 1991), and *Spiritual Monitoring* (Harper Collins, 1991), and a number of articles in *Review for Religious*.

Kenneth J. Galbraith is a counselor in spirituality and human development in Chicago. Ordained in 1960, he has his Ph.D. in English literature. Over the years he has held several administrative and teaching positions at Gonzaga University in Seattle. He was provincial superior of the Oregon Province of the Jesuits from 1970–1976. Then he was rector of the Jesuit school of Theology in Chicago until 1982.

Walter L. Farrell entered the Society of Jesus in 1934 and received his Ph.D. in philosophy from the Gregorian University in Rome in 1953. He taught philosophy for many years at West Baden College in Indiana and was rector there when this institution moved to Chicago as Bellarmine School of Theology. He was provincial superior of the Detroit Province from 1965–1971. He was in charge of formation at the National Jesuit Conference and was later president of that conference. He was director of the Spiritual Exercises Center at Colombiere Center in Clarkston, Michigan, and of the Romero Center at the University of Detroit. In the past he was, and more recently is now again, instructor of tertians for the Detroit Province.

Howard J. Gray entered the Jesuit order in 1948, received a number of degrees from Loyola University in Chicago, and pursued studies in English literature at the University of Wisconsin. He has held many administrative positions in the Jesuit order, including director of studies for the Detroit Province, rector of Loyola House in Detroit and of the Jesuit Community at Weston School of theology in Cambridge, Massachusetts, where he was later dean. He was provincial superior of the Detroit Province from 1983–1989, has been vice president of the Conference of Major Superiors of Men, and a consultant to the bishops of the Philippines. More recently he has been director of tertians for the Detroit Province and director of the Detroit Spirituality ministry team. But he is best known for the many retreats, lectures, and talks on Jesuit spirituality that he has given here and abroad.

Jules Toner entered the Jesuits in 1932, received his Ph.D. from the University of Toronto, and taught philosophy for many years at Loyola University, Chicago, University of Detroit, and at Bellarmine School of Theology in Chicago. He was director of novices from 1969–1972 for the

Detroit and Chicago Provinces. He has conducted many workshops on discernment of spirits in the *Spiritual Exercises* and other Christian spirituality programs. His publications include two books on philosophy, a number of articles and monographs in philosophy and Ignatian discernment, and two masterful tomes on St. Ignatius' Rules for the Discernment of Spirits and the individual discernment of God's will.

Peter Fennessy entered the Society of Jesus in 1957 and received several degrees from Boston College. He spent three years teaching high school in Jamaica and has been at John Carroll University since 1974 in campus ministry. Since 1986 he has been vice-president and director of the campus ministry team. He has published two articles on spirituality in *The Way*.

Shannon Barnes is currently director of the Internship for Spiritual Direction at Colombiere Spirituality Center in Clarkston, Michigan, a position that she has held for over ten years. She is a single parent of five children and received her M.A. from St. Thomas Theological Seminary in Denver. She has been involved in conducting workshops on spiritual direction and the *Spiritual Exercises* in many locales.

John A. McGrail entered the Jesuit order in 1928 and did his studies at Xavier University in Cincinnati and St. Louis University. He too held many administrative positions in the Jesuit order, including rector of West Baden College, provincial superior of the Detroit Province, rector of Colombiere Center in Clarkston, Michigan, pastor of Sts. Peter & Paul Church in Detroit, and president of Walsh Jesuit High School in Cuyahoga Falls. He too is best known, however, for the many talks and workshops he has given on spirituality and the *Spiritual Exercises*.

A special word of acknowledgment is due to the following who supported the lecture series which is the source of this book, both by their encouragement and by arranging for financial assistance for the series: Thomas W. O'Malley, S.J., formerly president of John Carroll University and now in the same position at Loyola Marymount University in Los Angeles; Michael J. Lavelle, S.J., formerly academic vice president at John Carroll and currently president; and Joseph E. Kelly, Chair of John Carroll's Religious Studies Department.

On references to the *Spiritual Exercises*, see the abbreviation list below. All scriptural quotations are from the New American Bible.

Abbreviations

A = The Autobiography of St. Ignatius, paragraph numbers. The edition cited, except where noted, is *St. Ignatius' Own Story: As told to Luis González de Cámara*, tr. William J. Young, S.J. (Chicago: Loyola University Press, 1980). (See Note 2 of ch 3.)

F = David L. Fleming, S.J., *The Spiritual Exercises of St. Ignatius: a Literal Translation and a Contemporary Reading* (St. Louis: The Institute of Jesuit Sources, 1978), page numbers.

[n] = All numbers in brackets are to the standard paragraph numbers of the *Spiritual Exercises*. Unless otherwise noted (e.g., in "F" references), the translation of the *Exercises* is that of Louis J. Puhl, S.J., *The Spiritual Exercises of St. Ignatius* (Westminster, Md.: The Newman Press, 1959).

1

The Centrality of Christ in
the *Spiritual Exercises*

Henry F. Birkenhauer, S.J.

Henry Birkenhauer's discussion of the Christocentric nature of the Spiritual Exercises *is a most apt way of beginning the reflections of this book. For it does much more than just get at the core of the Ignatian dynamic: it offers a fine summary of that dynamic and of the book of the Exercises. It provides as well clear explanations of some peculiar and historically conditioned terminology. Readers who have not had the opportunity of making the* Exercises *may find this particularly helpful.*

We need to know essential traits to distinguish gold from pyrites, an original from a copy, a true lover from a faithless friend. When does a retreat deserve the title *Spiritual Exercises?* Recently the Holy See published a document titled "Essential Elements of Religious Life." This list caused considerable debate but it also served to clarify the meaning of a term that has wide application.

So it is with the *Spiritual Exercises.* By the fact that they are meant to be adapted, various purposes are seen in them. William Peters, S.J., calls them a school of prayer. Hugo Rahner, S.J. (brother of the famous Karl), sees them as preparation for a choice; Thomas Green, S.J., sides with those who see discernment as essential. Joseph DeGuibert, S.J., believes that these authors are all seeing true aspects, different, yes, but rooted in the same reality. A study by Fr. Terrence Toland, S.J., poses and answers a question which is germane to our discussion.

How many characteristics might you derive from the Spiritual Exercises for Jesuit education? Some Scripture scholars tell us that if there were Magi who came to Bethlehem, a case can be made for 12 or 14 as well as three. Radical centrist that I probably am, I have opted to speak of the Ignatian vision in a traditional threesome: a purpose; a plan; and a preference for person.[1]

The purpose of the *Exercises* is the same as that of the Society of Jesus—to promote the greater glory of God. The plan is one of structure and flexibility. A quotation from Father Toland will help us:

> In every case the director is to let the retreatant go as far as he can, but always, always, the director is to let go and stay out of the way of the moving spirit of God. It is a daring resolution of the hendiadys, structure and flexibility, into structured flexibility. The major disease to be avoided is hardening of the absolutes. The operative key: adaptation to the individual's freedom in the Lord.

The third characteristic, a preference for person, is neatly summarized by Toland in this paragraph:

> I said at the start that the Spiritual Exercises are just that—a how-to manual, exercises to be made and not just read. I now round out the unfinished description. It is a how-to book for the journey, with other persons, to the Person sent by the Holy Trinity to conspire with his Holy Spirit in returning all creation to the Father. It is a journey leading to the Person, Jesus Christ.

For reasons which we hope to make clear in the remainder of this paper, we believe that "Christocentric" is the term which best describes the essence of the *Exercises*. This assertion does not mean that other retreat forms are not Christocentric. Rather we suggest that the *Exercises* assume that the pattern of Christ's life is the pattern for the growth and development of the spiritual life of the Christian. Starting from this Ignatian insight, all else follows in the *Exercises*.

Ignatius' *Exercises* are the story of his life.[2] Other saints have influenced generations through autobiographical accounts. He tells us what God taught him "like a schoolboy" in this little book of 370 paragraphs, which he edited, cast, and recast until it suited him.

His own life was Christ-centered. He would have the order which he founded called by no other name than the Company of Jesus. There was opposition, even in very high places, but Ignatius was adamant. And the name *Societas Iesu* has been declared, time and again, to be one of the substantial marks of his life-work.

A second indication of the Christocentric character of Ignatius' life is the prayer *Anima Christi*—in English, "Soul of Christ." An instruc-

tive article in the *Catholic Encyclopedia* states that this prayer has been
attributed to his authorship because he so frequently refers to it in the
Exercises and it is always given at the beginning of his text. Scholarship
establishes that this prayer was known to Christians at least two centuries
before the time of St. Ignatius. Clearly, though, it was one of his favorite
prayers. The *Anima Christi* is Ignatian in its brevity, its staccato cadence,
even its enumeration of various parts of Christ's body. The *Exercises* have
frequent classifications: thoughts, words, deeds in the examination of one's
conscience [32–42]; the three powers of the soul (memory, understanding, will) in meditative prayer [50 and 246]; persons, words, and actions
as a framework for contemplation [106–108]; the five senses [121–125 and
247]. The *Soul of Christ* was a prayer that Ignatius used, not just because
it responded to his tidy love of classification, but far more because it was
a little litany of Christ his Lord.

It remains for us now to show through the text of the *Exercises* that
"Christocentric" is truly the essence of the *Exercises*. So let us begin. The
first twenty sections, the Annotations, have numerous references to God
our Lord, God our Creator and Lord. These would apparently be references to God as Father. However, Annotation 4 [4], which gives the division of the retreat into weeks, states that "the second part . . . is taken
up with the life of Christ our Lord up to Palm Sunday inclusive; the third
part . . . treats of the passion of Christ our Lord; the fourth part . . . deals
with the resurrection and ascension." It is important to note clearly from
the outset that the "weeks" of the *Exercises* are not exact calendar references, but approximate periods or stages of greater or less length dependent on the needs of the one making the *Spiritual Exercises*. The first
"week" deals with sin and the retreatant's relation to the merciful Lord,
the second with the public life of Jesus, the third with his passion and
death, and the fourth with his risen life.

The "First Principle and Foundation" [23] of the *Exercises* seems to
be an abstract and more philosophical introduction to the *Exercises* and
completely bereft of any relation to Christ. Hugo Rahner, however, and
the host of scholars he refers to have shown that both this and the whole
of the First Week of the *Exercises* are implicitly rooted in Christ.[3] Indeed
for Ignatius even the term "our creator and Lord" referred to Christ and
his humanity. In this context, therefore, other apparently non-Christological
references to God in the *Exercises,* as mentioned in the preceding paragraph on the Annotations, are most probably in reality references to Christ.

A typical day in the First Week is outlined in paragraphs [45] to [72].
Here the Scripture background is definitely Old Testament in character
and the purgative way is the theological milieu. Yet in the midst of sin
and shame, the first exercise ends with this touching colloquy:

> Imagine Christ our Lord present before you on the Cross, and begin to speak
> with him, asking how it is that though He is the Creator, He has stooped
> to become man, and to pass from eternal life to death here in time, that
> thus He might die for our sins. I shall also reflect upon myself and ask:
> "What have I done for Christ?"
> "What am I doing for Christ?"
> "What ought I to do for Christ?"
> As I behold Christ in this plight, nailed to the cross, I shall ponder on what
> presents itself to my mind [53].

The third exercise of the First Week introduces a prayer technique,
often cited as characteristic of Ignatian methodology, the triple colloquy.
After combining the first two exercises, dwelling on the points of greater
consolation or desolation, the retreatant addresses Mary the Mother of God,
in a first colloquy asking for knowledge and abhorrence of sins. This petition is followed by a Hail Mary. Then comes the second colloquy:

> I will make the same petitions to her Son that He may obtain these graces
> from the Father for me. After that I will say *Soul of Christ* [63].

A third colloquy is made to God the Father.

The fifth exercise is one of the most striking in the entire text of the
Exercises—the meditation on hell. It is a kind of application of the senses
to the physical pains of the damned and its purpose is to deter from sin.
The final prayer, though in keeping with this blunt approach, is softened
by an appeal to Jesus:

> *Colloquy.* Enter into conversation with Christ our Lord. Recall to memory
> that of those who are in hell, some came there because they did not believe
> in the coming of Christ; others, although they believed, because they did
> not keep the Commandments.
> Divide them all into three classes:
> 1. Those who were lost before the coming of Christ;
> 2. Those who were lost during his lifetime;
> 3. Those who were lost after his life here on earth.
> Thereupon I will give thanks to God our Lord that He has not put an end
> to my life and permitted me to fall into any of these three classes.
> I shall also thank him for this, that up to this very moment He has shown
> himself so loving and merciful to me [71].

At the end of the First Week, Ignatius gives ten additional directions,
practical hints for prayer. The tenth is concerned with penance, a somber
subject, yet one distinctly appropriate to the purgative way. Speaking of
exterior penance (as distinct from interior penance—controlling our feelings and imagination) he offers three reasons for this type of mortifica-
tion. Reason 3 is germane to our purpose.

To obtain some grace or gift that one earnestly desires. Thus it may be that one wants a deep sorrow for sin, or to weep much over his sins or because of the pains and sufferings of Christ our Lord; or he may want the solution of some doubt that is in his mind [87].

Between the first and the Second Week comes one of the key meditations of the *Exercises*—the Call of an Earthly King. I will not give a detailed resumé of this striking and beautiful Ignatian parable which is part of the subject of chapter 5. Let me simply observe that with this transition to the Second Week the scriptural context is the New Testament, the spiritual climate is that of the illuminative way, and Jesus Christ is the subject and object of our prayer. It is within the last three weeks of the *Exercises* that the Christocentric essence becomes most explicit.

Following the meditation on the Call of the King, the Second Week properly begins with a contemplation on the incarnation [101]. The term "contemplation," as distinguished from "meditation" such as was used in the First Week, denotes affective prayer where acts of the will are given freer scope. In the First Week and in the Call of the King, the type of prayer is more discursive: ideas appeal to reason and rational conclusions are drawn. In the Second Week and throughout the remainder of the *Exercises*, the prayer is more intimate, more loving. A typical day will have two contemplations followed by two repetitions, followed in turn by an "application of the senses" in which the spiritual senses (the analogues of the bodily senses) are called into play.

Most important for our consideration, however, is the third prelude of each contemplation. In the Ignatian ascetic the first prelude recalls the history of the event (usually the scriptural account). The second prelude attempts to imagine the scene of the event. (Among the mystics, Ignatius uses the faculty of the imagination more freely than many.) The third prelude is a brief petition for the grace that the retreatant seeks. To illustrate, I quote the following third prelude from the contemplation on the incarnation.

This is to ask for what I desire. Here it will be to ask for an intimate knowledge of our Lord, who has become man for me, that I may love him more and follow him more closely [104].

We cannot overemphasize the importance of the third prelude. The "grace of the moment"—of this hour of prayer—is sought from the Lord. This form of third prelude will be used throughout the entire Second Week, varied only with the subject matter. For example, the third prelude for the Contemplation on the Nativity will be to ask for an intimate knowledge of our Lord, who has been born as a babe for me, that I may love him more and follow him more closely.

Every word in the *Exercises* was pondered, edited, and reedited by their saintly author. "To ask for what I desire" implies a deep, faith-driven yearning for a specific grace. "Intimate knowledge" is the language of one who is drawn by the cords of love. "That I may love him more"—the *magis* (more) seen elsewhere in the Exercises and in the Jesuit Constitutions— has all the connotation of a quest for excellence. "And follow him more closely"—could any request be more specific, more hope-filled, more loving?

This third prelude is prayed five times daily for nine days (the usual duration of the Second Week) and, with variations drawn from the subject matter, in the Third and Fourth Weeks as well.

A trait, though not the essence of the *Exercises*, is that they are developmental, a term meaning that the retreatant progresses step by step, not advancing until one has acquired the grace of the exercise in which he or she is engaged. The grace in question is precisely the one sought in the third prelude. No experienced director will allow a retreatant to continue until he or she is sure that the latter wants this grace with all his or her heart and shows signs that she has received it from the Lord.

Three days in the Second Week are spent in acquiring some ease in contemplative prayer. On the fourth day, the growth in contemplative knowledge of Jesus through the Gospels is seemingly interrupted with a return to discursive prayer. The Meditation on Two Standards is not really a digression. Rather, like a plateau, this complex reflection is a welcome pause, a chance to get one's bearings, to see in perspective what Christ's life really means to me.

Since chapter 5 will deal with this important meditation in detail, I shall only note that the Two Standards are really two military banners, one of Lucifer, the other of Jesus Christ, and that the grace sought in the third prelude is the following:

> This is to ask for what I want and desire. Here it will be to ask for a knowledge of the deceits of the rebel chief and help to guard myself against them; and also to ask for a knowledge of the true life exemplified in the sovereign and true Commander, and the grace to imitate him [139].

The meditation concludes with a triple colloquy: to Mary, to Jesus, to God the Father. As before, the second colloquy is addressed to Jesus and asks for the grace to imitate him better and concludes with the *Soul of Christ*.

An important Ignatian parable is proposed in the fifth period of prayer on the same fourth day [149–156]. Entitled "Three Classes of Men," it presents three levels of commitment to Christ. Omitting specifics, we simply note that the meditation concludes with the same triple colloquy as the Two Standards.

Following the fourth day, the retreatant continues with contemplations on the public life of Jesus Christ. Outlines for themes are given in an appendix provided by St. Ignatius [261–312]. He ordinarily divides the subject matter into three "points." Each contemplation is to conclude with the triple colloquy of the Standards.

Meanwhile another development is taking place in the soul of the retreatant. Knowledge and love of Jesus Christ will inevitably invite one to rethink the question asked in the First Week, "What ought I to do for Christ?" Answering this question may entail a choice of a way of life or a confirmation in a vocation already chosen. St. Ignatius prepares us for this with a special consideration, Three Kinds of Humility [165–168], which some have said is to the remainder of the *Exercises* what the Principle and Foundation was to the First Week.

To appreciate this consideration, we observe that "humility" in spiritual theology is not unadulterated self-abasement. Humility is honesty. Therefore the first kind of humility recognizes the truth of God's dominion over all creation and his consequent right to demand my observance of his law. From this disposition flows a firm resolve never to deny his sovereignty by committing a mortal sin.

The second kind of humility advances to a point where I see all creation as God's, not mine, and consequently am not inclined to prefer wealth to poverty, honor to dishonor, a long life to a short life if either alternative promotes equally "the service of God and the salvation of my soul" [166]. This is as far as the Principle and Foundation will take us.

Let us quote the description of the third step exactly as given by St. Ignatius:

> This is the most perfect kind of humility. It consists in this. If we suppose the first and second kind attained, then whenever the praise and glory of the Divine Majesty would be equally served, in order to imitate and be in reality more like Christ our Lord, I desire and choose poverty with Christ poor, rather than riches; insults with Christ loaded with them rather than honors; I desire to be accounted as worthless and a fool for Christ, rather than to be esteemed as wise and prudent in this world. So Christ was treated before me [167].

No Christian can read these words unmoved. They surely call us to the summit of perfection. The *Exercises* can lead us no higher. Indubitably, they are Christocentric. And to complete this consideration, St. Ignatius adds the following note:

If one desires to attain this third kind of humility, it will help very much to use the three colloquies at the close of the meditation on the Three Classes of Men mentioned above. He should beg our Lord to deign to choose him for this third kind of humility, which is higher and better, that he may the more imitate and serve him, provided equal or greater praise and service be given to the Divine Majesty [168].

From paragraphs [169] through [189], the retreatant is invited to choose a way of life, if that choice is still open, or to reform "one's way of living in his state of life." This is the method of election, or discernment of the will of God, so famous in the *Exercises*. This discernment is not the same as that of discernment of spirits to be treated in chapter 6.

The third kind of humility is a perfect preparation for the Third Week of the Exercises. Some authors, e.g., Fr. Thomas Green,[4] suggest that the third kind of humility could be logically incorporated into the Third Week which calls us to follow Christ in his passion and death. In this week the third prelude of each contemplation is described as follows:

This is to ask for what I desire. Here it will be to ask for sorrow, compassion, and shame because the Lord is going to his suffering for my sins [193].

There are six points for prayer in each contemplation of the Third Week; the first three propose seeing the persons, listening to their conversation, and observing what they are doing, respectively. The remaining three help us to see the Christology of the *Exercises*. We quote them in full:

Fourth Point. This will be to see what Christ our Lord suffers in his human nature, or according to the passage contemplated, what he desires to suffer. Then I will begin with great effort to strive to grieve, be sad, and weep. In this way I will labor through all the points that follow.

Fifth Point. This is to consider how the divinity hides itself; for example, it could destroy its enemies and does not do so, but leaves the most sacred humanity to suffer so cruelly.

Sixth Point. This is to consider that Christ suffers all this for my sins, etc., and what I ought to do and suffer for him [195–197].

The colloquy which concludes the contemplation is directed, of course, to Christ, but the vocal prayer at the end is the Our Father, not the Soul of Christ, as we might expect. One opinion holds that Jesus' Agony in the Garden, and indeed the entire passion, derives its spiritual force from the petition, "Thy will be done," in the Lord's Prayer.

Paragraphs [289–298] of the appendix offer a division of the passion into ten episodes of three points each. In the body of his text, Ignatius distributes these "mysteries" over six days with a midnight meditation, a second mystery on all days but two, two repetitions, and an application of the senses. The seventh and last day of the Third Week is a *dies luctus,* a day of grief, in which the entire passion is reviewed at the side of Mary and the apostles [208].

An interesting addition to the Third Week is the insertion [210–217] of the Rules for Eating. Commentators see this as a practical application of Christian asceticism introduced at an appropriate time.

The Fourth Week deals with the risen life of Jesus, beginning with an appearance of Christ not recorded in Scripture. St. Ignatius is terse, almost impatient, as he writes,

> He appeared to the Virgin Mary. Though this is not mentioned explicitly in the Scripture it must be considered as stated when Scripture says that he appeared to many others. For Scripture supposes that we have understanding, as it is written, "Are you also without understanding?" [299]

With the change in subject matter comes a new third prelude:

> This will be to ask for what I desire. Here it will be to be glad and rejoice intensely because of the great joy and the glory of Christ our Lord [221].

To the three points customary in Ignatian contemplation (persons, words, actions) two additional Christological aspects, proper to the Fourth Week, are added:

> *Fourth Point.* This will be to consider the divinity, which seemed to hide itself during the passion, now appearing and manifesting itself so miraculously in the most holy resurrection in its true and most holy effects.
>
> *Fifth Point.* Consider the office of consoler that Christ our Lord exercises, and compare it with the way in which friends are wont to console one another [223, 224].

A single colloquy is prescribed, concluding, as in the contemplations on the passion, with an Our Father.

The Ignatian Notes to the Fourth Week help the retreatant to rejoice in the Lord. Ignatius has stated [10] that the purgative way "corresponds to the exercises of the First Week," and that the illuminative way "corresponds to the exercises of the Second Week." The unitive way, third and highest of the classical "ways" of prayer, is not specifically mentioned, though the mysteries of the passion, death, and resurrection of Jesus can and surely have prepared souls for special graces of contemplation.

After the contemplation on the ascension, and surely in the spirit of the unitive way, comes the great Contemplation to Attain the Love of God

[230–237]. Following the best scholarship on the *Exercises*, "God our Lord," to whom this prayer is addressed, in the context of the theology of the *Exercises* as a whole is the incarnate Word, even though Christ is not explicitly mentioned.[5]

Saint Ignatius includes the Three Methods of Prayer [238–258] as a substantial part of the *Exercises* [4]. In these techniques, designed to vary prayer experience, especially, we think, for the tired and overworked, the prayer *Soul of Christ* is mentioned twice [253 and 258].

From our brief survey of the *Spiritual Exercises*, we trust that the importance of the Life of Jesus is evident. Without Christ, we should have simply a series of methods of prayer and some perceptive techniques of discernment. With Christ, the *Exercises* live. We have called the *Exercises* Christocentric in the sense that they focus on Christ whose life is the paradigm of the life of every Christian.

Through Christ the Christian is born, grows, seeks the will of the Father. With Christ, suffering acquires meaning and purpose. In Christ we die, we live again, we reign in heaven forever. If Christ is the center of our lives, from him radiate, like the spokes of a wheel, the stages of growth and development of every Christian. Our lives may form a perfect circle around Christ as did Mary of Nazareth, Mary of Magdala, John of Capernaum, Ignatius of Loyola. The Christian grows through Christ, with Christ, in Christ. That is why the essence of the *Exercises*, the *anima*, the vivifying principle of their enduring life, is that they are indelibly Christocentric.

NOTES

[1]This and the following two quotations are from unpublished manuscripts of Terrence Toland, S.J., of the staff of the Maryland Province of the Society of Jesus. They are used with permission.

[2]See Walter Farrell's contribution, "The Background of the *Spiritual Exercises* in the Life of Ignatius," ch 3, below.

[3]Hugo Rahner, *Ignatius the Theologian*, tr. Michael Barry (New York: Herder and Herder, 1968). See ch III, "The Christology of the *Spiritual Exercises*" and especially 61–67 and the references there in footnote 18.

[4]Thomas H. Green, S.J., *A Vacation with the Lord* (Notre Dame, Ind.: 1986). 144–145.

[5]Rahner, 134–135.

2

The Cultural Milieus of
the *Spiritual Exercises*

Tad Dunne

Tad Dunne's contribution is aptly titled. Note the plural of milieu. But the plurality of milieus is not merely the historical one of Ignatius' time, but the very pertinent intersection of the Spiritual Exercises *with our current spiritual preoccupations. The first part showing the background of the reform of the Church at Ignatius' time is easily correlated to different kinds of need for reform today. Ignatius' desire to reform the lives of the influential is transferred not primarily to the growing predominance of the laity today, but, more fundamentally, to the need for group as distinguished from individual or "Lone Ranger" effort at reform. The second part on the warfare spirituality allegedly so characteristic of the* Exercises *is correlated not only with its Patristic roots in Augustine, et al., but also with the interior conflicts Freud and others have apprised us of in recent times. Perhaps, the most stunning of Dunne's correlations between Ignatius' background and the cultural situation in which we find ourselves, is the original insight he proposes in the third part of his lecture between Ignatius' strange silence on the Holy Spirit and what we today ought to identify as the genuine object of that often maligned devotion, to the Sacred Heart of Jesus.*

Imagine that tomorrow you will be visited by a short, wiry Rumanian poet who has spent the last fifteen years walking across Russia in search of the wisest men and women he could find. You will have a few hours to spend with him, talking about his poetry. Presumably most of us would feel both intellectually curious and intellectually exposed: curious to ask about the experiences behind his written word, but exposed to the light which his poetry casts on our unnoticed assumptions. Still, we trust that an honest sage would grant us copious benefits of doubt and gently lead us to uncover wisdom beneath our clumsy questions. A genuine seeker of truth would sidestep our curiosity about himself and stand beside us—the three of us: ourselves, the poet, and the poetry—to address the mystery of life together.

So it is with looking at the cultural influences on Ignatius as he wrote the *Spiritual Exercises*. We cannot simply look "behind" his text to understand its origins. The hermeneutics of a classic is a two-edged sword. As we scrutinize the cultural setting in which it was born, a classic can simultaneously scrutinize the present cultural assumptions behind our questions. But the circle of scrutiny is not closed; it can spiral upwards and uncover new paths for action. After all, what is the worth of wisdom if not for some concrete effect? Indeed, the *Exercises* I am talking about refer not primarily to the book Ignatius wrote but to the four "weeks" of prayerful calisthenics designed to release a man or woman for action.

Three questions in particular strike me as possessing this power to reveal the assumptions both of Ignatius and ourselves and to carry us beyond our cultures as they are to what a future culture might be through the instrumentality of the *Exercises*. First, how important is it to wed the *Exercises* to the reform of the Church? Second, is war still the best metaphor for the spiritual life? And third, why the great silence about the Holy Spirit?

The Exercises *and Church Reform*

First, then, let us look at the atmosphere of Church reform within which Ignatius conceived the *Exercises*. Beginning from the twelfth century, the social fabric of the Western world was tearing apart. The Black Death of 1348 killed one out of three Europeans. The recurring encroachments of the Ottoman Empire and the Hundred Years' War rearranged ancient political allegiances. The vast social organization of Christendom was breaking up into rival nationalisms.

The Church itself was in tatters. During the Great Schism (1378–1417), three popes simultaneously claimed the chair of Peter. While Ignatius was growing up, Pope Alexander VI was dedicating himself to the pleasures of the flesh, then Pope Julius II to politics, and then Pope Leo X to the arts. The organizing power of a Thomistic theology based on faith was now competing with a humanism based on reason. Monasteries had grown rich, to the resentment of the populace, while popes and clerics sold bail bonds on purgatory. This selling of indulgences was not merely the clergy's sin; it also represented a fanatically superstitious Christian population beset by a Satanic fever.[1]

It is one of the recurring paradoxes of history that when people fear evil spirits, they are also dazzled by the order of the spirits, to the extent of shunning the restraints of law and authority. Beginning with Joachim of Flora in the late twelfth century and the Franciscan Spirituals after him, many Christians longed for a future Church of pure Spirit, where pope, sacraments, and Church laws would no longer be necessary.[2] In the fourteenth century Meister Eckhart taught an exalted mysticism, and the Rhine Valley "Friends of God" sought to live out lofty spiritual ideals. As we might expect, these anti-Church sentiments helped shape the spirit of many Protestant reformers.

Of course, there were also many attempts to mend the ragged fabric of the Church. The Council of Constance (1417) ended the Great Schism. The Fifth Lateran Council (1512-17) attempted to clarify doctrine and end abuses (unfortunately not enforced by Leo X) and the Council of Trent (1545-63) largely succeeded in doing so.

Another reform movement had arisen far from Rome. Late in the fourteenth century, owing to the preaching of Gerard Groote and the founding of the Brethren of the Common Life, a lay movement sprung up in northern Europe known as the *Devotio Moderna*.[3] It deliberately worked to break down the medieval barriers of law and custom that existed between the clergy and the laity. It put education more in the hands of lay women and men, thereby raising the dignity of lay discipleship throughout Europe. Thus we have Thomas More, Catherine of Sienna, Joan of Arc, and Frances of Rome. Born as it was during the Western Schism, it is understandable that the *Devotio* fed upon a certain alienation from the hierarchical Church. Besides, since the focus of its reform was chiefly on a personal conversion of life and not on a programmatic reform of communities in the Church, it remained marked by its individualistic tone, and this in turn seemed to imply that an organizational Church and communal living were evil or at least unnecessary—an offensive thought for clerics and monks.[4]

Where the *Devotio Moderna* relativized the clergy, a later movement, the Clerks Regular, reformed them. Beginning in 1524 with the Theatines, an Italian community dedicated to the intellectual formation of priests, clerks regular abandoned Office in choir, the habit, and obligatory penances. They took no vow of stability, and therefore, because they expected to be on the road and out of sight of superiors, they looked to the vow of obedience to bind them together. Among the half dozen or so congregations of clerks regular that were founded by 1550, the Society of Jesus became the most famous and was known at the time to have been founded specifically for the reform of the clergy.[5]

In the face of the general breakdown of wisdom and the outbreak of fantastic spiritualisms, there also emerged a felt need for discernment and prudence. Gerson, chancellor of the University of Paris (d. 1429), wrote a work called "Test of Spirits." Citing a phrase from Ignatius of Antioch, he said, "Counterfeit and genuine coins are being circulated. God's money and the devil's money are being passed around; and what is most needed at the present time is, according to our Lord's word, 'expert money changers.'"[6] Bonaventure, too, gives rules for discernment in his *De Processu Religionis*. Clearly, Ignatius carried on this tradition in his rules for discerning which he included in the book of the *Exercises*.

Finally, we can only mention the most enduring and traumatic attempt at reform: not a mending but a hemming of the separated pieces—the sectarian reforms of the fifteenth century and the great Protestant Reformation of the sixteenth.

By the middle of the sixteenth century, we find Jesuits, whose central formative experience was the *Exercises*, at the center of Church reform, shaping the ecclesiology of the Council of Trent and opening up a number of colleges for the education of clergy—first for their own numbers and then for others preparing for ordination. So it would appear that Ignatius ultimately used the *Spiritual Exercises* for the reform of the Church, particularly through the instrumentality of reformed orders. For centuries afterwards, religious and priests were practically the only people who made them, and the general effect was more to deepen their personal devotion to Christ and their readiness to maintain Church institutions rather than to prepare them to preach the Word of God to the unchurched.

But if Ignatius were sitting here learning about our culture and the Church's mission today, would he still advise that we keep our eyes strictly on revitalizing Church personnel? Perhaps he would educate us in how to use the *Exercises* by telling us how he first conceived them. At no time between his conception of the *Exercises* (1521) and the founding of the Society (1540) did he show any concern with reforming the structure of authority in the Church. Nor, on the other hand, was he content merely to bring individuals to conversion. His aim was to create apostles—men and women who respond to the call of Christ our Lord, "who chooses so many persons, apostles, disciples, etc., and sends them throughout the whole world to spread His sacred doctrine among all people, no matter what their state or condition" [145].

True, about five years after his experiences at Manresa, as Ignatius weighed several different ways of helping souls, he considered entering a corrupt order for the express purpose of reforming it (A 71). True, he was ordained and did found an order of "reformed priests." But by his own account, he often speaks of wanting to study in order to help souls more effectively[7] without ever mentioning a vocation or a desire to be a priest. He did not want to *be* anything: he wanted to *do* something.

Owing, most likely, to the terrible reputation of monks and to rising hopes in a reformed clergy, Spanish Inquisitors insisted that only a priest could exercise leadership in the Church. So, during the years between 1522 (Manresa) and 1528 (to Paris), Ignatius' desire to help souls became concretized in his choice to become a cleric himself.[8] He gathered a group of reformed priests around him, and proposed that they begin catechizing in the Holy Land. In this project, the *Exercises* were to be their primary tool. At this time, he wrote to his confessor, "The *Spiritual Exercises* are the best means I can think of in this life both to help a person benefit him/herself and to bring help, profit, and advantage to many others. Even though you felt yourself to be in no special need, you will see how they will help you serve others beyond anything you ever dreamed of."[9]

The Mediterranean war against the Moslems prevented them from travelling to the Holy Land, so, following a contingency plan, they presented themselves to the pope to be sent wherever he thought most expedient. Because of the desperate need for an educated clergy at the time, the Society of Jesus quickly became what it remained for centuries: intellectually prepared educators for the Church.

As with all of us, historical circumstances directed Ignatius with a far firmer hand than his personal desires alone ever could. His yearning to "help souls" by means of the *Exercises* had to be backed-up by clerical training, and the desires he shared with his first clerical companions had to be put at the disposal of the pope. But for all these historical eventualities, we should not lose sight of the fact that just as Ignatius meant the *Exercises* for apostolic enablement and not merely individual conversion, so he meant them to revitalize the entire People of God, not merely the Church's ecclesiastical personnel. The mobilization of a group of reformed priests was merely the concrete and timely strategy to free the energies of "so many persons, apostles, disciples, etc., . . . to spread His sacred doctrine among all peoples, no matter what their state or condition."

If Ignatius conceived the *Exercises* primarily for those people most likely to have an impact on the world, then we should consider our assumptions about who these people might be today. Some commentators have suggested that the *Exercises* ought to be given more to the laity, since their influence in both the Church and in secular society seems to be growing. While this may be so, it overlooks a deeper shift, not in *who* wields influence but in *how* they wield it. In the Western world, the most "influential" people are no longer strictly rich, clerical, or titled individuals. What counts nowadays is teamwork, democratic processes, organizing, ongoing feedback and revision, and negotiating on behalf of a constituency. It has become increasingly unrealistic to give the *Exercises* in such a way that the kind of apostle emerging from them is a spiritual "Lone Ranger." Instead, they ought to shape men and women who expect to collaborate no matter which vocation they have followed in the Church. Specifically, the *Exercises* should be given to groups who already work as a team, who pin their effectiveness precisely on group effort, being careful to preserve, however, the very private dealings between God and the individual which Ignatius insisted on.[10] In other words, our eyes should turn not from priests and religious to the laity, but from effective individuals to effective groups.

Influential people today are also far more educated than they were in Ignatius' time. In North America, Catholics are the largest group of educated Christians; their college education stands above national averages. As we might expect, more and more educated men and women are being drawn into the *Exercises*. What is often overlooked, however, is what effect the *Exercises* should have on their professions. In Ignatius' time the *Exercises* empowered a person to minister in a practical, pastoral world with a Christian vision. Today, however, educated Christians recognize that faith expresses itself in work for justice, and justice, in turn, requires the long-range views and the theoretical work of political science, psychology, and economics.

The *Exercises*, in fact, do convey an image of the human person that stands in direct opposition to much of what is taught in the human sciences. For example, Ignatius' views on how our desires for riches and honors lead ultimately to a self-defeating individualism run opposite to the liberal ideal of the self-made person. Also, his easy assumption that we can purposefully and responsibly exercise any feelings we please certainly has a place in modern psychology, which tends to regard clients as slaves, not as masters, of their own feelings. Educated retreatants, therefore, can expect to reenter their intellectual or professional lives with a critical vision gained through making the *Exercises*.

Here, however, Ignatius might advise us that collaboration and critical vision do not by themselves actually detach people from the values that actually govern their behavior. Today, materialism, consumerism, and sexism distort our vision and constrict our fields of action in ways we hardly notice. To be genuinely healed of this inner blindness requires a conscientization, an overcoming of fear and apathy, and a willingness to let go of anything for the sake of the Kingdom. It is no small work to achieve this detachment. Compared to this difficult inner liberation, collaboration and critique are a piece of cake. But this is where the *Exercises* do their best work, bringing retreatants to detest the sins and biases that entrapped them, and giving them a Spirit-driven Jesus to imitate.

As far as this detachment goes, our times are not much different from Ignatius' times. But when we look at how to direct the energies released by this detachment, our world of collaboration and critical vision open up new possibilities which, paradoxically, are closer to the evangelical purpose of the *Exercises* and less identified with reforming Church personnel. Frankly, I think Ignatius would be wide-eyed with excitement over these uses of the *Exercises* which our culture has made possible.

A Warfare Spirituality

If Church reform is not at the core of the *Exercises*, what about its warlike spirit? The entire structure of the *Exercises*, commentators say, is built on the highly militant parables of the Kingdom and the Two Standards.[11] Their polemical features were not Ignatius' own invention, but a development of an ancient tradition. During the convalescence which led to his conversion, he was reading "The Golden Legend," a book on saints' lives by Jacopo de Voragine.[12] In the section on St. Augustine's "City of God," he read:

> That book was concerned with the story of two cities, with the kings of these two cities, Jerusalem and Babylon. For Christ is king over Jerusalem, Satan over Babylon. Two contrary loves gave birth to these cities. The city of Satan was built on self-love, mounting up even to contempt of God; the city of Christ was built on love of God, mounting up even to the contempt of self.[13]

This text gave Ignatius an immediate contact with the originating Christian tradition of the warfare spirituality classically formulated by Augustine's theology of history.[14]

In the Middle Ages, Augustine's militant spirituality had become supercharged by the spirituality of the crusades. Although the last great crusade ended in 1291, the desire to push the Turks back from Europe continued deep into the time of Ignatius. It engendered a strong belief that God called one to leave home on a crusade, to share in the incarnational work of Jesus in poverty—drafted, as it were, into the militia of the Kingdom of God with a readiness for martyrdom rivaled today only by the Iranian ethos of Holy War. Although much appeal was made to the spiritual benefits of a crusade—the chance to do penance for one's sins and to contribute to "the glory of God" against infidels—it also ignited papal hopes that its own temporal power over civilizations could be restored.[15]

Ignatius grew up in this militant spiritual/political atmosphere. In 1469, Ferdinand and Isabella had united Spain after two hundred years of clan feuds. Months after Ignatius was born, Spanish royal consorts pushed the Moors from Granada, their last strong outpost in Spain, thus making an eight-hundred-year-old dream come true. His own father participated in a crusade against the Moors, and his brother died in one. Ignatius himself longed for free passage to visit the Holy places "perpetually" (A 45). But when historical circumstances forced him and his companions to abandon their hope of helping souls in the Holy Land and to direct their efforts instead to letting the pope tell them where best to serve, Ignatius then seems to have redirected all the style and energy of a crusader into the interior life.

While today we may admire this spiritual transformation of the crusader ideal, none of us can repeat it. The political ideals of Ignatius' day gave him a symbol of dedication, loyalty, and self-sacrifice that reinforced his spiritual vision. But I believe that the reigning political ideals of our own time, while they provide our spiritual lives with an equally dominant symbol, work against us as an apt metaphor for the spiritual life. Our international attitude of balance of powers seems perfectly matched by a spiritual attitude of peaceful coexistence of inner desires, no matter where these desires are directed. Today's popular psychological wisdom runs: "Tolerate everything that arises from consciousness" in the same style that liberal democracy refuses to denounce alien values. Suppression of hostile forces in the psyche is called sickness, and some Eastern spiritualities counsel befriending one's demons. What, then, are we to make of this militant spirituality of the *Exercises?*

Again, Ignatius might answer us by pointing to his experiences. A look at his *Autobiography* reveals that he did allow as much as possible into consciousness; it is full of astute observations on his spontaneous thoughts and feelings. If his spirituality is warlike, it lies in keeping close watch on the doors of the subconscious and, like an attentive guard at the castle gate, inquiring, "friend or foe?" of all interior movements. If foe, then he deliberately drives out the images and feelings invading his inner sanctum.[16] The problem with today's popular wisdom is not the allowance of unnoticed feelings but the extreme tolerance to being moved by them, as if they represented one's truest self.

Transposing Ignatius' practice into the categories of Freud's unconscious, I believe that Ignatian spirituality today should teach ways of keeping a moral distance between (1) the spontaneous thoughts, images, or feelings that occur in us and (2) our responsible choice either to cooperate with them or suppress them. Failure to guard my own gate results in too easy an identification of my person with the feelings that rise up in me, the images that capture my attention, and the inner voices that distract me from other inner business. I end up regarding my own person as bad when I only feel bad or becoming overconfident when my head is swimming with images of success. In either case I am not living in the truth of my soul, having been invaded and captured by forces that entered unchallenged. So there is good reason for taking a militant attitude in the spiritual life, although not one that shoots everything that moves. It is rather the militancy of an immigration official guarding the homeland of one's psyche.

Silence on the Holy Spirit

My final question is perhaps the most provocative. Why is there such little mention of the Holy Spirit in the *Exercises?* Ignatius seems to downplay the Spirit's work in a number of contemplations on the life of Christ and to omit the Spirit's role entirely in others. One would think he would be especially reluctant to excise the Spirit from the crucial contemplations on the annunciation and the temptations, but this he does.[17] There is nothing on the Holy Spirit in his Rules for Discerning Spirits nor in any "annotations." In his only direct reference to the Holy Spirit, Ignatius is absolutely cautious:

> I must be convinced that in Christ our Lord, the Bridegroom, and in His spouse the Church, only one Spirit holds sway, which governs and rules for the salvation of souls. For it is by the same Spirit and Lord who gave the Ten Commandments that our holy Mother Church is ruled and governed [365].[18]

One reason for Ignatius' silence may be that the ideal of "Imitating Christ" overshadowed any tendencies he might have had towards a spirituality of "Obeying the Spirit." He seems to have inherited the practice of contemplating the Life of Christ from the *Devotio Moderna,* perhaps from Jan Mombaer (d. 1501), who wrote "A Rosary of Spiritual Exercises and Sacred Meditations," which was used at Montserrat, or from a similar book of exercises written by its own abbot, Garcia Jimenez de Cisneros (d. 1510). In these exercises, one contemplated the personality, style, and virtues of Christ in order to model one's behavior after him. So, in his *Exercises,* Ignatius focuses quite strictly on the humanity of Jesus, skipping all the parables, and all but five of his miracles. In about forty-four of the fifty scriptural passages he gives for contemplation, a retreatant is expected to *walk* somewhere with Jesus, engaging in conversation "exactly as one friend speaks to another" [54].

The spirituality of Imitation has an ancient lineage. It can be found in the *Didache* (written about time of John's Gospel) and in Ignatius of Antioch (d.c. 107).[19] With St. Francis, the ideal became popularized but narrowed to imitating Christ chiefly in poverty. Ignatius was likely influenced by the Franciscan reform that took place at Arevalo, where, at fifteen years of age, he was assigned to the royal court.[20] But more than this, *The Imitation of Christ*, the greatest classic emerging from the *Devotio Moderna*, was held dear by Ignatius from the earliest days of his conversion.

Remember that Ignatius was far more apostolic, far more devoted to the Church, and far less individualistic than the ideals of either the *Devotio* or St. Francis would warrant.[21] Still, he accepted without question that the actual life of the historical Jesus was meant to reveal how the most meaningful life looks in the flesh:

> Those who are progressing in the spiritual life and truly following Christ our Lord love and intensely desire . . . to suffer injuries, false accusations, and affronts, and to be held and esteemed as fools . . . because of their desire to resemble and imitate in some manner our Creator and Lord Jesus Christ.[22]

Notice that he regards Christ as "Creator." For Ignatius, the very Creator of Humanity came expressly to show us how to walk.

It is doubtful, however, that the spirituality of the Imitation of Christ could have so completely overshadowed the role of the Holy Spirit in the *Exercises* were it not also for a "Spiritphobia" spooking the Church at the same time. Not that this is anything new. From the very beginnings of Christianity, many Churches have shown a great fear of the Spirit. For example, where Luke and John depict Christ giving the Spirit to guide the Church, Matthew has Christ say, "Behold, I am with you all days," leaving the Spirit entirely out of the picture. Perhaps the reason for Matthew's silence can be found in Paul. If we read his letters chronologically, we find decreasing mention of the Spirit, diminishing to zero in his letter to the Colossians.[23] Judging by his troubles with charismatics in Galatia and Corinth, it seems plausible to assume that Paul, and then Matthew, were unable to control the problem of private inspiration by the Holy Spirit of God within an institutional Church.

One solution was to channel the work of the Holy Spirit strictly along official lines, emphasizing that the Holy Spirit is given chiefly to Church authorities and not just to any disciples. This is the route followed by Luke (but not John).[24] A more psychological solution was to distinguish between the gift of discernment coming from the Holy Spirit and the various personal inspirations which come from good or evil "spirits." This too has some scriptural warrant, at least as far as the work of the Holy Spirit is concerned. There is little clear evidence in the New Testament that the Holy Spirit is said to deliver a new message to anyone. Instead, the Spirit helps people decide between known options. In other words, the "inspiration" by the Spirit does not reveal facts; it reveals values among the known possibilities which inspire people.

This is also the route followed by Ignatius. In the Constitutions and the Formula of the Institute, he usually portrays the Holy Spirit as giving someone a vocation (at root a value judgment, not a factual message) or as inspiring wise choices.[25] But he had to watch his tongue. The Inquisition was putting the heat on anyone who claimed to have the Spirit in any sense whatsoever. When a Dominican friar once accused Ignatius of speaking through the Holy Spirit, he said of himself, "the pilgrim kept cool at this" (A 65).

Nowadays, there seems to be less reason than ever for silence about the Infinite Spirit of God in the *Exercises,* provided we remember that the Holy Spirit acts like an umpire, not a messenger. Paul says that the love of God has been poured forth into our hearts (Gal 5:5), that this produces faith, which is "the eye of the heart" (Eph 1:18), which discerns good and evil in the everyday. In other words, we should take seriously Paul's statement that it is the Holy Spirit who gives the power to discern between different spirits (1 Cor 12:10; 1 Cor 2:14-16).

There are a number of places in the *Exercises* where we can recognize and call upon the Spirit. In the examination of conscience and the examination of meditation, where Ignatius tersely recommends that we ask God for light, we should specifically ask God as Infinite Spirit to give us an eye for the truly worthwhile. And we should thank God as Spirit for those junctures in our day where we knew which path to take and which to avoid. In fact, any time we try to "discern the spirits" that move within us, whether during a retreat or in everyday life, we should ask the Holy Spirit to give us divine perception for which movements are worth admitting into consciousness.

Likewise, in our contemplations on the life of Christ, it is precisely the Holy Spirit that gives us our appreciation of Christ, our attraction to Christ, and our desire to be like Christ. Of course, our imagination can present an ungenuine Christ, so we cannot be certain that all our images or thoughts about Christ are trustworthy, but we can trust that the Spirit, both in us and in the Church, wants to uncover the real Christ and eventually to expose any false illusions.

But besides calling on God as Spirit for these various times of discernment, we can also recognize and learn about the Spirit at work in the very life of Christ as we contemplate its various scenes. Discerning the Spirit in Christ will mean a certain transformation or development of the highly Christological tradition of the Imitation. But I doubt that the pinnacle of Imitation lay in merely imitating how Christ behaved externally. Primarily it is an imitation of how he listened within, using his visible behavior as a test case of the limits of self-sacrifice. "Have that *mind* in you which was in Christ Jesus," Paul says, describing the general pattern of Christ's inner obedience.

In a daring commitment to an eleventh century reinterpretation of Christ, the Society of Jesus in the seventeenth century looked deeper into Jesus the itinerant preacher to find something more at the core of love to imitate, namely, through devotion to his Sacred Heart. Obviously, by "heart" here no one meant the fluid pump in the chest of Jesus; his Sacred Heart stood for the wellspring of divine values, sensitivity, and compassion that moved him. Yet this is exactly what Paul referred to as the Holy Spirit. Dogmatically, then, the time has come to proclaim a fundamental equation about Christ: the Sacred Heart of Jesus *is* the Holy Spirit. When we contemplate the love that drove Christ into the desert; that taught, healed, and gathered companions; that cried, "Abba, Father!"; and that gave himself up to the forces of evil rather than compromise his vocation, it is precisely the Holy Spirit whom we contemplate.

So far I have talked about liberating the *Exercises* for their original purposes of apostolic enablement and about maintaining the proper militant attitudes towards the thoughts and feelings that strike us. But the idea of introducing the Holy Spirit into the very texts of the *Exercises* ought to give one pause. Might this be tinkering with an organic masterpiece that should be left intact? Would Ignatius allow it?

Two considerations prompt me to stand by my suggestion. First, Ignatius in fact adapted the *Exercises* in many ways himself, depending on the situation of the retreatant. Retreatants today do not experience the great fear of spiritualisms that dominated Ignatius' time. Today, we have greater insight both into the psychology of discernment and into Scripture to hold us in good stead. Besides, we would not be overlooking anything in the *Exercises* but merely filling out their meaning with a view of the Holy Spirit which Ignatius clearly expressed elsewhere.

My second consideration, however, seems not merely to allow God to appear as Spirit but to demand it. It is a matter of doctrinal integrity and orthodoxy. God sent two saviors, two "helpers," not one—the visible Christ Jesus in our history and the invisible Divine Spirit in our hearts. It is theologically impossible to gaze on Christ Jesus without also seeing the Infinite Spirit of Christ and the Father, albeit often unrecognized. Silence may have been necessary during a time of rampant confusion about the Spirit's role, but continuing that silence today verges on practical heresy—something Ignatius would abhor.

When I first made the *Exercises*—twenty-seven years ago now—I was given Louis Puhl's red, hardbound version. I still have it here, with masking tape holding the spine in place and numerous underlinings inside. Time and time again, I have marveled at the genius of Ignatius lurking behind the words. But, of course, the point of these particular words has been to liberate me from my own compulsions, making me a malleable instrument in the hands of God. Keeping that purpose utmost in mind as our principle of adaptation, I believe we can give the *Exercises* in a way that both hears the language of Ignatius and speaks powerful words today.

NOTES

[1]Dom Francois Vandenbroucke, "Lay Spirituality from the Fourteenth to the Sixteenth Century," part 2, ch 9, of Jean Leclercq, ed., *The Spirituality of the Middle Ages* (New York: The Seabury Press, 1982) 490.

[2]Hugo Rahner, *The Spirituality of St. Ignatius Loyola* (Chicago: Loyola University Press, 1980) 78. See also "Spiritualism" in *The Westminster Dictionary of Church History*, Jerald Brauer, ed., (Philadelphia: Westminster Press, 1971) 784-5. For the effect of Joachism on the Jesuits, see Marjorie Reeves, *The Influence of Prophecy in the Later Middle Ages: A Study in Joachism* (Oxford: Oxford University Press, 1969) ch 9, "Jesuits," 274-290.

[3]For a list of main features of this movement, see Thomas Clancy, *An Introduction to Jesuit Life* (St. Louis: Institute of Jesuit Sources, 1976) 29-30.

[4]Michael Foss, *The Founding of the Jesuits 1540* (New York: Weybright and Talley, nd) 55-6.

[5]Clancy, 18-20.

[6]Rahner, 79-80. An early directory on the *Exercises* cites this phrase.

[7]See A nos. 29, 45, 50, 54, 63, 70, 71, 85. See A 93 and 95 for his only references to ordination and A 85 for a significant omission of the fact.

[8]See J. William Harmless, "Jesuits as Priests: Crisis and Charism," *Studies in the Spirituality of Jesuits* 19/3 (May 87) 1-47 for an insightful discussion of Ignatius' rather instrumental notion of priesthood.

[9]Letter to Manuel Miona, Venice, 11/16/1536 in William J. Young, ed., *Letters of St. Ignatius of Loyola* (Chicago: Loyola University Press, 1959) 27-8.

[10]See [15] and Javier Osuna, S.J., *Friends in the Lord* (London: The Way Series, 1974) no 3, 52-3.

[11]Rahner, 53.

[12]The Golden Legend, or *Flos Sanctorum*, was written in Latin by a Dominican in the thirteenth century and translated into Spanish by a Franciscan during Ignatius' childhood—1493 and again in 1511.

[13]Rahner, 28.

[14]Of course, God gave Ignatius an extraordinary insight into the struggle of the human soul represented by this parable, and Ignatius made his own contribution to the dialectic, particularly in his Francis-like love for poverty and his more clearly apostolic thrust.

[15]Hans Wolter, "Elements of Crusade Spirituality in St. Ignatius" in F. Wulf, ed., *Ignatius of Loyola: His Personality and Spiritual Heritage, 1556–1956* (St. Louis: Institute of Jesuit Sources, 1977) 97–134.

[16]He clearly regards them as coming "from without": See [32, 326, 327, 351]. See my "Extremism in Ignatius of Loyola" *Review for Religious* 45/5 (September–October, 1986) 345–355. Compare this to the fifth-century Diodochus of Photiki who takes for granted that "the heart produces good and bad thoughts from itself" and then struggles with the question of how both good and evil thoughts can come out of a person. He will not go so far as to say that the "Holy Spirit and the devil dwell together in our intellect." See *The Philokalia*, trans./ed. by G.E.H. Palmer et al., vol I (London: Faber & Faber, 1979) 284–5 (nos 83–5). See also Evagrius the Solitary, "Texts on Discrimination regarding Passions and Thoughts," *ibid.* 38–52, especially no 23, 52. He pits demons against both the Holy Spirit and personal virtue. There is no mention of good spirits.

[17][262, 263, 268, 273, 274]; see also the brief mentions in [304] and [312] about Jesus giving the Holy Spirit.

[18]See a similar remark to Teresa Rejadell in Young, *Letters*, 22.

[19]See Rahner, 70. In the New Testament, Paul speaks of imitating Christ mainly in his death. Only as the canon of Scriptures was closing did the ideal of imitating Christ as a model of life become a part of Christian tradition.

[20]*Ibid.* 18–20.

[21]*Ibid.* 55–57, 87.

[22]From the "General Examen" no 44. See George Ganss, ed. *The Constitutions of the Society of Jesus* (St. Louis: Institute of Jesuit Sources, 1970) 108.

[23]I am using the following set as the order of authentic letters of Paul: 1-2 Thessalonians, Galatians, 1-2 Corinthians, Romans, Philippians, Colossians. I consider Ephesians, where the Holy Spirit reappears, as a disciple's more orderly recap of Pauline theology without the restrictions of practical concerns of local situations.

[24]This is also the strategy of Pope John Paul II. His *Dominum et vivificantem* (1986) repeatedly depicts the passages from John's Gospel as a gift of the Holy Spirit to Church authorities—"apostles" in the place of "disciples" (nos 3, 5, 6, 22, 23, 25, 42). He cites the Spirit's work as principally in ordination and secondarily in confirmation, mentioning charismatic gifts only once (no 25). See *Origins* 16/4 (June 12, 1986) 77–102.

[25]Formula of the Institute, nos 3, 4; Constitutions of the Society of Jesus nos 134, 414, 624, 697, 700, 701; in George Ganss, ed. *The Constitutions of the Society of Jesus* (St. Louis: Institute of Jesuit Sources, 1970). In some letters, Ignatius does spell out some roles played by the Holy Spirit in guiding a person, mainly through the gifts of prudence, wisdom, and consolation. But see, in particular, Young, *Letters*, 95, 205, 258.

3

The Background of the *Spiritual Exercises* in the Life of St. Ignatius of Loyola

Walter L. Farrell, S.J.

Walter Farrell correlates the events of Ignatius' conversion experiences at Loyola and Manresa, the profound illumination at the Cardoner, and Ignatius' interpretation of those experiences, with key points in the dynamics of the Spiritual Exercises. *Then the genesis of the text of the* Exercises *itself, elaborated later, is connected with those early discernment experiences. The outcome is an insightful subordination of what is secondary to the essential in the book of the* Exercises, *which many have often found confusing.*

The previous chapter dealt with background, the atmosphere or socio-cultural setting within which St. Ignatius lived. This chapter too deals with background but the term here is understood quite differently, since we will be speaking of how the *Spiritual Exercises* emerged from the lived experience of St. Ignatius. The hope is that the very tracing of this genesis will provide us with a window through which we can more easily catch a glimpse and come to understand the central meaning of these *Exercises*.[1]

Two preliminary remarks may be in place before we go ahead with the development of our thesis. The first is that, although there is a difference in the understanding of background in these first two chapters, a real continuity should also be noted. That is, the third dimension mentioned in the last chapter as part of the ecclesiastical culture of the day was fear of the Holy Spirit. To anticipate what will be coming in this chapter, however, one could say that the *Exercises* as Ignatius conceived them were not built on fear but rather trust of the Holy Spirit. This is a trust that recognizes the Spirit to be at work in our world and that the discov-

ery of this work of the Spirit by Ignatius is an unwritten premise underlying his own life and the whole of the *Exercises.*

A second preliminary remark deals with things we will not be doing
in this chapter. For example, there is no intention of presenting a biogra-
phy of St. Ignatius here; in fact, we will not be touching whole segments
of his life at all. Again, we will not be doing a literary study of the *Exercises* or trying to identify parallels in other writers of the time to passages
in the book of Ignatius. Nor is ours going to be a study of the text of the
Exercises or of the history of the manuscript tradition. Lastly, we will not
be dealing with every detail and part of the book of the *Exercises.* This
is true not only because other parts of the book will be treated in some
detail in later chapters but also because our focus will be on the genesis
of the *Exercises.* We will be studying the graced experience of St. Ignatius
with a view to highlighting the central dynamic of the *Exercises,* which
is captured in a relatively small set of materials in the book. But we are
running ahead of ourselves. Better that we turn to the life of Ignatius and
try to locate ourselves.

St. Ignatius of Loyola lived from 1491 to 1556. There is some dispute
about the year of his birth but the vast majority of scholars now take the
year 1491 as the proper date. For our purposes, however, we can begin
our considerations with 1521. Obviously, the previous thirty years left their
imprint on Ignatius, as the previous chapter has shown, but for our purposes in treating the genesis of the *Exercises,* we can safely take our beginning date as May 1521, when Ignatius was wounded at Pamplona and
taken to the castle of Loyola to recover. It is there that his "new life" began.
On the other end, we need not reach out all the way to 1556 but can consider 1534 as a fairly reliable end-date for our investigation. We have the
copy of the *Exercises* that the companion of Ignatius, Peter Faber, had.
It dates from 1534 and it is substantially what we have today. In a word,
as the following diagram shows we need concern ourselves only with a
small segment of the life of Ignatius.

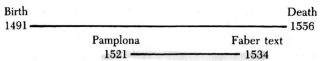

Birth		Death
1491 —————————————————		1556
	Pamplona	Faber text
	1521 —————————	1534

But even this shortened period can be further broken down. And, at
the risk of running ahead of our presentation of evidence, it may be helpful to further divide this shortened period of Ignatius' life under consideration. It has been the tradition, and scholars have only confirmed its factual
accuracy, to say that the *Exercises* in some way are the result of the unique
graced experience of St. Ignatius at Manresa. He stopped at Manresa after

he left Montserrat, intending to pause but a short time. That time expanded into some ten or eleven months and constituted what writers have called Ignatius' "long retreat." Hence, it is not inappropriate to divide the period of 1521–1534 into three: the key Manresa period which is central, flanked by Pre- and Post-Manresa periods. In diagram form it would look like this:

Pre-Manresa	Manresa	Post-Manresa
1521-1522 ————————	1522-1523 ————————	1523-1534

The two diagrams are helpful in locating us in time in the life and experience of Ignatius, but they can also be misleading. The movement, for example, in each diagram is linear and it is from left to right. It can lull us into the belief that the development of the *Exercises* was linear and a matter of straight-line progression. Here again, our tripart division of the 1521–1534 period is helpful if we also recall a simple experiment done in the physics laboratories of our high school days. Remember how we scattered iron filings on a piece of paper and then brought a magnet under the paper. Presto! The filings immediately assumed a new look and took on a discernible pattern around the poles of the magnet. In keeping with the imagery of the experiment, the reader should try to conceive the various experiences or events in Ignatius' Pre-Manresa life as well as those in the first part of his stay at Manresa, as the iron filings. Initially, they were for Ignatius, as we will see, but disparate elements or occurrences in his life.

Now try to imagine the last part of the Manresa time, and especially the Cardoner Vision (so-called) as the magnet brought to these disparate elements with an effect parallel to that of a magnet on filings. The disparate elements suddenly become intelligible; Ignatius has a key insight of his life. In terms of the *Exercises,* their core and dynamic are made apparent. However, there certainly were additions to the disparate elements now integrated and patterned by the magnet of Manresa and, hence, there is a Post-Manresa time. These additions are just that: material that Ignatius added to supplement, complement, or expand the central material of the *Exercises.* If one were drawing a picture of the filings affected by the magnet, then, some circles around this picture could be used to capture this last period in the development of the *Exercises.*

We have spent a bit of time developing the image of filings and magnet because it is important to recognize right from the beginning that the *Exercises* of St. Ignatius did not develop in a straight, linear fashion any more than they came straight from heaven, as one pious tradition would have. To think of them otherwise would be as unfortunate as thinking one can readily understand the *Exercises* by just picking up the book and reading it.

But let us come back to our time frame. We narrowed the time in Ignatius' life down to the period from 1521–1534. In turn, we divided this period into three segments: the Pre-Manresa, the Manresa, and the Post-Manresa. Using the parallel of the physics lab experiment with iron filings and a magnet, we have indicated that each of these segments calls for a different treatment. It is now time to take up each segment and we will use as a guide in this study what St. Ignatius himself provides us with in his *Autobiography*.[2]

I

The events that are recorded in chapter 1 of the *Autobiography* are few. We learn that Ignatius is brought back to the ancestral castle for recuperation from his wounding at Pamplona. It was found necessary to reset his shattered leg, in the course of which process he almost dies. There follow some ten months of recovery during which Ignatius did a good bit of reading, reflecting, and praying. Finally, in March 1522, he feels he is sufficiently recovered and decides to begin a pilgrimage to Jerusalem. But this chronological recital is quite inadequate for capturing what Ignatius experienced during this Pre-Manresa time.

Let us turn to these experiences, but before doing so, it may be good to remind ourselves that the *Autobiography* is an unusual composition. It might well be thought of as anticipating what scholars today call oral history. For in producing it, Ignatius would talk to one of his contemporaries, Father De Camara, and the latter, once they had finished a conversation, would run to his room and try to write down as close to a verbatim as his memory would allow. Such is the way the *Autobiography* was put together. There is a time factor involved here also. The conversations and their "recording" all took place toward the very end of the life of the Saint. For our purposes, then, we must remember that we are hearing reflections of Ignatius on his past and, even more important, that we are getting a selected set of such reflections. We will come back to this point later but for now it is good at least to advert to it.

We know from the *Autobiography* that Ignatius' first choice in reading material was novels but, when none of these could be found in the castle, he settled for reading the *Life of Christ*, by Ludolph of Saxony and the *Golden Legend*, a collection of lives of the saints made by Jacopo de Voragine.[3] Two complementary experiences emerged from this reading. First, after reading for a bit especially in the lives of the saints, Ignatius would daydream a bit about what he would do when he had recovered.

These daydreams were, as he acknowledges, of the brave deeds of a knight and feats of arms that would win the heart of a fair lady. At one point he noticed both similarity and difference between the reading and the daydreams: both were engaging and pleasant while going on; afterward, however, in the case of the reading a peace and quiet consolation obtained while the aftermath of the day-dreams was distaste and restlessness. As Ignatius notes himself, he merely caught the fact of this difference without any realization at the time of its meaning or significance (A 8ff.).

The reading also led the saint to a real fascination with and love for the life of Christ and the Gospel stories recorded by Ludolph. Eventually this led the saint to begin a notebook in which he recorded (carefully, as he says, and using red ink for the words of Jesus and blue for those of Mary) the passages that especially struck him (A 11). Again, the *Autobiography* notes only the fact without any indication that this could be the beginnings of the directive in the *Exercises* that the retreatant in repetitions go back to the place in the text that proved to be the most attractive in previous prayer.

The third experience of Ignatius at Loyola was one of enlightenment which led to the need for a decision. This decision, in turn, brought him to a whole new direction in his life. Readings in the lives of Christ and the saints faced Ignatius with an outlook on life that was quite different from the one that had been guiding him up to that time. He recognized the clash between this view and the view that had prevailed for him earlier. He came to see the sinfulness of his earlier way and became a real penitent. Indeed, he saw his life open out: first, to a pilgrimage and, then, to a possible life in a monastery where he could live the rest of his life in atonement. It was Ignatius the penitent, then, that we see at the end of the first chapter of the *Autobiography* who puts aside the entreaties of his brother and resolutely sets out for Barcelona where he would begin his pilgrimage (A 12).

II

The rather humorous incident which he recalled for De Camara regarding his conversation on the road with a Moor is indicative of Ignatius' stage of conversion. His old instincts told him to defend the honor of the Blessed Virgin; his new outlook prompted him to take another approach. His experience by his own admission was of being unable to resolve the matter. Instead, rather simplistically, he drops the reins on the neck of his donkey and allows the animal's choice at a fork in the road to determine his action. On reflection in his *Autobiography*, Ignatius simply records the facts of the story and lets them speak for themselves (A 15). Obviously, for him, as he looked back on the event from the end of his life, the story spoke of not knowing how to make an appropriate decision in his newly chosen way of life.

One thing that Ignatius did have well in hand, however, even at this point, was his sense of being a sinner and his need—because such a sinner—to become anonymous, just a pilgrim. This led him to Montserrat where he planned to discard the clothes of Ignatius of Loyola and don the garb of Inigo the pilgrim, to make a general confession, and to hold a vigil of arms. We are not exactly sure when Ignatius arrived at Montserrat. Since his vigil was on the night of March 24–25, 1522, and he took three or four days to make his confession, as he tells us, it seems reasonable to suppose that he arrived around March 18, 1522. Like other pilgrims, he was given a place to stay, to pray and prepare for confession. He was also given at least the Purgative Way part of the *Ejercitatorio* by Garcia de Cisneros.[4] Unlike others he was finally allowed through the good services of his confessor, Jean Chanon, to rid himself of his donkey and make an all night vigil before the feast of the Annunciation.

We can only guess at the experiences of Ignatius during these days because the *Autobiography* contains no comments from him about his interior state or dispositions. His prayer of preparation for and his making of a general confession, we can presume, could only have deepened his sense of sinfulness; similarly, we would assume, that the symbolism of making a vigil of arms in his new found service would have been as exhilarating as any vigil of arms he might have made before.

A final point before we conclude this segment of our study deals with what has only been alluded to earlier, namely, the anonymity of the pilgrim that Ignatius desired. It would seem from a reading of the *Autobiography* that Ignatius had not only become aware of his sinful past but had also conceived a kind of hatred of his ways in the past. He associated sinfulness with the style of life he had led and with typical thoroughness had a strong desire not only to rid himself of sin but of the lifestyle that he felt had led him along the way to sin. From a knight of some renown he wanted to become an unknown, a kind of a nothing, since he felt that this was precisely what he deserved.

Again, Ignatius symbolized this for himself by, first, getting rid of the Loyola clothes he was wearing and putting on the traditional pilgrim's garb he had bought. Secondly, he rid himself of his beast by giving it to the monastery, which became complicated since he wanted to remain anonymous as a donor. Thirdly, as he set out from Montserrat on March 25, 1522, he realized that despite walking on foot and his wearing new garments, he could still be recognized by some of the people coming on the feast day to the monastery. Hence, he turned off the main road for Barcelona and after a short journey came to Manresa where he decided to remain a few days until the feast-day travelers had gone their way. There is an obvious doggedness in this that is typical of Ignatius, the man of strong desires and resolute execution. The stop at Manresa, however, lengthened out well beyond a few days and it was only in late January or early February 1523 that Ignatius set off again for Barcelona. Let us turn to the Manresa days and the central events and experiences out of which the *Exercises* emerged.

III

The life of Ignatius in the early part of his Manresa stay would be described by spiritual writers as one of active asceticism.[5] He set himself a regimen of begging alms, abstinence from meat, and considerable prayer. The latter included daily participation in the Church's Eucharistic prayer and the public Liturgy of the Hours as well as some seven hours of private prayer. Finally, there was the matter of personal appearance. In the past Ignatius had been fastidious in this regard, so now he decided to counter his concern by a deliberate neglect. He let his hair and his nails grow and in general presented an unkempt appearance.

In all of this the saint was experiencing the elation that is often called "first fervor." As the *Autobiography* tells us, these early days at Manresa were days of consolation and considerable peace. Despite the severity of his daily round, he lived life with serenity and a consistent happiness. He notes especially the consolation that he experienced from a bright object that used to appear to him. While he had no idea what the object was and could not describe it with any clarity, the longer it was present the more intense was the consolation he derived from it.

As with anyone in "first fervor," however, the saint also experienced some difficulties. He tells us of the thought that came to him on occasion which ran: "How can you stand a life like this for the seventy years you have yet to live?" He tells us that he was able to dismiss the temptation quite successfully by simply countering with the statement that he could not promise himself even an hour of life and hence would leave all in the hands of God. With this the temptation left and the peace and happiness continued undisturbed (A 20). It might be good to note here as we have earlier that Ignatius noted only facts from his experience during these early Manresa days. On his own admission, he noted the fact of a sequence between the bright object and the temptations of which we have just spoken. He records the fact that the temptation seemed to follow on the appearance of the object but, as with other observations, he carried the matter no further. No questions of meaning or implications occupied him at this time.

This "first fervor" of Ignatius ran on some three to four months but then, as he notes in his *Autobiography*, rather suddenly things started to change. The months of fervor were followed by a very turbulent period of perhaps a couple of months. There was no change in the regime that had been set, but his interior started to change considerably. He speaks of the rapid alternation of consolations and desolations. At one time he would sense a strong consoling joy and then it would be taken away like a cloak torn off one's back. He found going to personal prayer or liturgies to be very tasteless. He sought people who would converse with him about the things of God with a hope of finding some help. No help was found; no relief came. Indeed, matters got worse.

One of the practices that was standard for Ignatius every Sunday was confession. At this time there began to slip into his confessional preparation questions about his general confession at Montserrat: had he confessed everything; had he given the confessor an accurate picture of this or that sin? The unrest here quickly spread from Sunday and confession preparation to every day. He became tortured with scruples and, as usually happens with scrupulous people, the more he examined matters the worse they got. Nor did his confessor really help him when he said that he should confess only things that were clearly sinful, for this only increased the problem by forcing an already scrupulous person to decide what was clear. Matters moved to the extreme, as the *Autobiography* notes, when Ignatius thought of throwing himself into a cistern to end his life and the torment in which he was living (A 22-24).

Then, it happened. All human helps had failed Ignatius, and so he turned with renewed insistence to God. Then, after confession one Sunday, there was a peace which continued into Monday, but by the next day the plaguing questions started anew. But at this point for the first time Ignatius noticed that such questions could not be of God because they distracted him and interrupted his relationship with God. He decided then and there to put them firmly aside and not to review them any more. The scruples dissipated; peace returned. Ignatius had a first glimpse of what one might call the "principle of discernment." Now let us note the difference here between this and earlier experiences. Previously, Ignatius was aware of facts, like those just recorded; here, however, the very nature of the experience involved his catching some of the meaning embedded in the facts, namely, the meaning of discernment.

What spiritual writers might characterize as the "dark night" was ended for Ignatius and with it the last part of his stay at Manresa began. His pattern of life was altered somewhat. For, while prayer time remained the same, some of the penance was moderated. Further, an apostolic dimension of "outreach" also appeared in his life. He began to attend again to his appearance lest it turn people away, and he also continued to seek out people with whom he could talk about the things of God. Now, however, he was not so much seeking help for himself as seeking to help others. This "help of souls" became a mark of his spirituality for the rest of his life.

The central experiences of this third period at Manresa were mystical. The *Autobiography* records five of them. Obviously, all of them had their impact on Ignatius but for the purposes of this chapter it will be helpful to concentrate on only one, the famous "The Vision of the Cardoner." The Ignatian experience on the banks of the Cardoner river is described in the *Autobiography* this way:

> He was once on his way, out of devotion, to a church a little more than a mile from Manresa, which I think was called St. Paul. The road followed the path of the river and he was taken up with his devotions; he sat down for a while facing the river flowing far below him. As he sat there the eyes of his understanding were opened and though he saw no vision he understood and perceived many things, numerous spiritual things as well as matters touching on faith and learning, and this was with an elucidation so bright that all these things seemed new to him (A 30).[6]

The last three sentences of the citation are of central importance for us, and they each deserve some comment. "[T]he eyes of his understanding were opened," Ignatius tells us. Despite the fact that writers and preachers continue to speak of the vision of the Cardoner, pretty obviously Ignatius had no vision. He does speak of "eyes" but they are the eyes of the understanding that are opened. The next sentence underlines this same point for it says: "[H]e understood and perceived many things, numerous spiritual things as well as matters touching on faith and learning." Ignatius did not see but his understanding was expanded. Was this a mystical grace? Biographers and other authors dealing with this part of Ignatius' life would unanimously affirm it was. It was a mystical grace not encased in a vision but rather a gift of understanding. However, the final sentence comes in here saying: "[A]nd this was with an elucidation so bright that all these things seemed new to him." Ignatius is telling us that his experience of enlightenment was not just a matter of bringing some further clarity to a particular point or two but that it was an expansive illumination that transformed everything in his life and that in such a way that all "seemed new." Silos has studied the Cardoner experience in some detail and makes the convincing case that the illumination of the Cardoner was what we might today call an insight and, as with any radical insight, this insight put a new face on everything because things were now seen from a new perspective.[7] As Silos points out, the insight Ignatius caught was the centrality of the principle of discernment.

One thinks here of the famous incident in the garden when Helen Keller was working with her teacher and caught the insight into language. That is, beyond the simple association of signs with objects, with which she was already familiar, of a sudden her mind was opened to the possibility of using signs to convey meaning and from this insight the meaning of language was born for her. Something similar was experienced by Ignatius at the Cardoner. He suddenly caught on to the idea that happenings in his life (especially the affective happenings) could have a meaning. They could be of God; they could also be from other sources. He realized that God indeed did act in people's lives and that if this action of grace were "read" properly, one could both detect God's action and the direction which God might be inviting one to follow.

As we bring to a close this part of our study, we might recall the example of iron filings that we used earlier. We have in the preceding pages looked at a number of individual events that took place in the Pre-Manresa and the early part of the Manresa periods. These events are like so many iron filings, to use our figure. Then in the last part of the Manresa stay, we came on the great illumination Ignatius received when praying on the banks of the Cardoner. In terms of our figure, this graced illumination is the magnet in that it opened Ignatius' eyes, threw light on the preceding events of his life, interrelated them and made them all seem new. The illumination at the Cardoner was a basic insight in which Ignatius caught the principle of discernment and in light of this principle many events or happenings in his life that he had noted but had not previously understood fell into place.[8] Indeed, he was able to bring this principle to bear on subsequent events in his life in such a way that he could say toward the end of his life that the Cardoner vision taught him more than all else put together. This would not necessarily have meant that it was richer or deeper than the vision of LaStorta but it could mean that the intelligibility afforded by the illumination of the Cardoner pervaded his life; it gave him a methodology and affected his ways of thinking to an extent that no other single event in his life ever did.

Indeed, with the illumination of the Cardoner, Ignatius' whole thinking, not just about events and discernment, changed, but also his understanding of Jesus and the mission of Jesus changed. It was as if the jottings in red that he had made in his notebook of a sudden took on a whole new look. Leturia, cited by Hugo Rahner, makes this point explicitly when he says:

> Above all, the ideal of the King and the Two Standards, with which Inigo was already familiar even before this date, takes on a wholly new meaning

in the whole of this constructive refashioning of the *Spiritual Exercises.* At Loyola he saw in Christ the eternal King only a model for imitation, and the example of His great-hearted sufferings evoked loving sympathy in him as it did in the saints all down the centuries. But now this King became for him a living person, actively exerting his influence today and yesterday, with the mission entrusted to Him by His Father not yet wholly completed, and seeking therefore, today and yesterday, for generous co-fighters and friends desirous of showing themselves faithful companions in arms.[9]

In light of the Cardoner experience, then, Ignatius could see that God's action was a consistent call and invitation that looked for and expected a response. History, especially the history of sin, showed that the movement from call to response was difficult; the road of continued and consistent response to call was anything but smooth. Evil, strident voices, and divergent invitations were constantly interfering with efforts at a faithful response to call. All of this put Jesus' life in a different light. It was not just a beautiful example that served as a model; it was more a mission, something to do. Jesus had entered on the task but it was as yet incomplete. Hence, disciples are invited to complete the mission with Christ. It is in a sequence of thinking of this kind that one can catch such parts of the Exercises peeking through: the Kingdom, the Election, the Two Standards, and the like. All of this brings us to the last part of our study, the application of what we have seen in terms of the book of the *Exercises.*

IV

The groundwork has now been laid. We have attended to a number of events in the life of Ignatius from his days at Loyola through his time at Manresa. We have taken an extended look at the key event in all of these Ignatian experiences, that is, the illumination at the Cardoner. We are now in a position to understand the implications of all of this for the genesis of the book of the *Exercises.* We can now rather briefly indicate when and where various parts of the *Exercises* emerged. Let us begin with the period that was central to the development of the *Exercises.*

1. *Manresa:*

We spoke at the end of the previous section about Ignatius' insight into discernment and his shift of thinking about the life of Jesus. These provided him with a view of the disciple as one called (1) who, despite difficulty (2), can recognize God's call and respond (3). There are guiding principles (4) that facilitate response and especially there is the inspiration of Jesus' life to live on mission with him (5). Expressed in terms of the book of the *Exercises,* we find, then, that the following parts emerge during the Manresa period:

> The Call of the King (Kingdom) (1)
> The Two Standards (2)
> The Election (except for the introduction) (3)
> The Rules for Discernment (4)
> The Rules for Scruples (4)
> The transformed view of the life of Jesus which obviously affects the selection of scenes from Jesus' life to be proposed to the exercitant. (5)

In a word, while some of the material in the above parts of the *Exercises* comes from the Pre-Manresa period, the core of the *Exercises* (the five parts numbered above), comes with and from the central experiences of the Manresa period itself. Ignatius himself is our witness here for prior to Manresa he does not talk of the *Exercises* but after Manresa, even before the addition of many other important materials, he does speak of "the book."

2. *Pre-Manresa:*

Here we deal very little with specific parts of the *Exercises.* If there are such, they are three or four at most:

> Examens: particular and general
> Methods of prayer (some)
> Confession
> [Some would add here the First Week meditations on Sin, etc.]

Certainly, there are other things that happened in the Pre-Manresa period that have a part in the development of the *Exercises,* but they do not enter the book directly. For example, the importance and the impact of the life of Jesus began for Ignatius at Loyola but it was only the transformed sense of Jesus' life that found its way into the book. Similarly, Ignatius had noted at Loyola the difference between his interior experiences after reading from the lives of the saints and after daydreaming. However, as Pre-Manresa events they were merely noticed; they were what we have called disparate elements. They were only understood when the light of the Cardoner illumination was turned on them.

Then, there are the First Week meditations on Sin and Hell, Death, and Judgment, about which I have raised a question by inserting the material in brackets above. This issue is a much larger one than can be handled adequately here but a few words may not be out of place. Certainly, one can find ideas in the *Exercises* on sin, hell, death, and judg-

ment that clearly seem to have parallels in the *Ejercitatorio* of Cisneros
that Ignatius used at Montserrat. Similarly, in putting together his First
Week material there seems to be little doubt that words, phrases, and sentences in the *Exercises* reflect Ignatius' familiarity with Cisneros' work.
But one would be hard put to find in Cisneros something like the first
meditation of the First Week of the *Exercises,* i.e., what is often called
a meditation on the history of sin. Hence, too, one finds no parallel to the
significant sequence Ignatius suggests with his first two exercises on sin.
For, he does not ask the retreatant to start with personal sin but proposes
that the retreatant see personal sin (second exercise) within and as part
of the history of sin (first exercise). The contention can be made, then,
that (a) the mechanics on the history of sin is an outgrowth of the same
Ignatian experience at Manresa that gave rise to the Two Standards and
(b) that the reason it precedes personal sin and ends in a colloquy with
Christ crucified is because in light of the Manresa experience, the mission of Jesus is seen at work in the historical struggle with sin and evil.[10]
In a word, while some elements of First Week material are definitely Pre-
Manresa in origin, the central structure of the Week and some of its characteristic features reflect the experiences of Manresa and their transforming effects.

3. *Post-Manresa:*

One could summarize here quite simply by saying that all the other
parts of the book of the *Exercises* emerged in the Post-Manresa period.
However, it may be useful to spell this out a bit more. True, not everyone
agrees with all that follows but, for the most part, what is stated here is
common currency with the classical studies on the *Exercises.*

a. From Ignatius' time at Alcala and Salamanca come:

The Principle and Foundation
The Introduction to the Election
The Sin Meditations (reworked)

b. From Ignatius' time in Paris come

A General Revision of "the book"
The Presupposition
The Annotations (at least the first half of them)
The Additions
The Three Classes
The Three Modes of Humility
The Contemplation to Obtain Love

The Rules for Almsgiving
The Rules for Thinking with the Church (at least in part)
Mysteries in the Life of Christ
The Rules for Eating (?)

c. From Ignatius' time after Paris

The Annotations (the rest, some would say)
The Rules for Thinking with the Church (the rest, some would say)

Some might place other elements here but most would think of post-Paris changes as only further refinements of the same basic material.

V

Now that we have come to the end, what has been achieved? It is hoped that the chapter has allowed the reader to see:

a. the key elements Ignatius chose to put into his *Autobiography* (and some authors would see the elements as deliberately selected by Ignatius to highlight what for him was an extended discernment brought to an extraordinary conclusion at the Cardoner);

b. that the reader has been enabled to see how the various parts of the *Exercises* grew out of, emerged from, the life experiences Ignatius presents in the first chapters of the *Autobiography*.

But, especially, it is also hoped that the overall presentation has allowed the reader to understand what is central to the *Exercises*. Having such an understanding one can approach them properly; not having a grasp of what is clearly central to the genesis of the *Exercises* gives rise to distortions in the use of the *Exercises* themselves. For example, if one just opens the book and starts to read one might sense that the first substantive item is the Principle and Foundation and conclude that the whole of the *Exercises* is an unfolding of the Principle and Foundation. Indeed, people have made a case for this. But from what we have said, this is clearly a misreading since the Principle and Foundation was composed some time after Manresa and after the time when Ignatius is talking of having "the book." If nothing else, our study should not only help to avoid this misreading but it should lead people to think of the Principle and Foundation itself in a different way or, at least, to ask why Ignatius composed it in the post-Manresa period when what Lainez refers to as "the substance" of the *Exercises* was already in hand at Manresa. One could make a similar comment about the *Contemplatio*, which some have written about as the goal Ignatius aimed at in composing his book. Again, there is a sense in which the *Contemplatio* is a summary exercise but it is a misreading of the origins and history of the text to think of it as the guide to Ignatian authorship.

To conclude, then, with a renewed emphasis. The *Exercises* facilitate a specific type of retreat and prayer experience. Central to them is the Cardoner insight about discernment: being aware of God's action and striving to ascertain the lead of God's Spirit in one's life. Hence, first and foremost they are a way of choosing to follow Jesus in his mission (and of offering to help complete that mission) and to do this in the specific way that Jesus' Spirit leads. They could be described as a method of setting the conditions of possibility for one to receive the (mystical) grace to serve.[11]

NOTES

[1]Two classic studies on the genesis of the *Exercises* are Leturia, "Genesis de los Ejercicios y de San Ignacio y su Infligo en la fundacion de la Compania," *AHSI*, vol 10 (1941) 16–59, and H. Pinard de la Boullaye, *Les Etapes de la Redaction des exercises*, Paris, 1950. To which can be added the shorter piece by Iparraguirre in his introduction (13ff) to the *Obras Completas de San Ignacio de Loyola*, B.A.C., Madrid, 1952.

[2]There are a number of editions in English of the *Autobiography*, but those edited by John C. Olin (New York: Harper Torchbooks, 1974) and Joseph N. Tylenda, S.J., (Wilmington: Michael Glazer, 1985) have the advantage of a good introduction and excellent footnotes. The Olin edition, however, does not retain the paragraphing numbers from the original edition as other editions do.

[3]On these books and their influence on Ignatius, see Pedro Leturia, S.J., *Inigo de Loyola*, tr. Aloysius J. Owen, S.J., Syracuse, 1949, 22ff.

[4]For more detail in these days at Montserrat, see Leturia, *op. cit.*, 23ff.

[5]For a fuller development of the Manresa experience in terms of ascetical and mystical experience, see Adolf Haas, "The Foundation of Ignatian Mysticism in Loyola and Manresa," (Centrum Ignatianum Spiritualitatis [C.I.S.] publication, vol XIII, 1982, no 39–40) esp. 164ff.

[6]The translation here is that of Joseph Tylenda. See note 2 above.

[7]Leonardo R. Silos, "Cardoner in the Life of St. Ignatius of Loyola," *Archivum Historicum Societatis Jesu*, vol 33 (1964) 3–43.

[8]Cf. citation from Polanco (MH Chin. Pol., I, 20) in H. Rahner, *The Spirituality of St. Ignatius*, tr Francis Smith, Chicago, 1980, 53.

[9]Leturia cited in H. Rahner's *Spirituality*, 54.

[10]Cf. The use Pope Paul VI made of the questions in the First Meditation Colloquy [53] in his opening talk to the delegates of the XXXII General Congregation of the Society of Jesus, December 3, 1974.

[11]Still one of the best brief presentations of the service dimension of Ignatius' spirituality and its place in the Exercises is in the Introduction to *The Jesuits: Their Spiritual Doctrine and Practice. A Historical Study*, by Joseph De Guibert, Chicago, 1964.

4

Christ and the First Week
of the *Spiritual Exercises*

Howard J. Gray, S.J.

Howard Gray succinctly presents to us (1) an overview of the First Week of the Exercises, *(2) the centrality of Christ in that week and the consequent emphasis on redemption rather than the more popularly proposed and consequently misunderstood emphasis on sin, and (3) the relation of the First Week to the rest of the* Spiritual Exercises. *It should also be noted that his explanation of the week as both a structure and a movement rather than a period of exactly so many days is equally applicable to the other three "weeks" of the* Exercises.

Introduction

For many the chief, if not exclusive, encounter they have had with the First Week of the *Spiritual Exercises* is the third-chapter narration of a Jesuit retreat in *A Portrait of the Artist as A Young Man*. James Joyce has given us a masterful parody of the *Exercises*, a parody, unfortunately, too often enacted not in the pages of fiction but in the presentation of the *Exercises* in actual pastoral situations. You recall that Joyce's protagonist, Stephen Daedalus, enters his three-day preached retreat convinced of his own sinfulness:

> He had sinned mortally not once but many times and he knew that, while he stood in danger of eternal damnation for the first sin alone, by every succeeding sin he multiplied his guilt and his punishment. His days and works and thoughts could make no atonement for him, the fountains of sanctifying grace having ceased to refresh his soul . . . What did it avail to pray

when he knew that his soul lusted after its own destruction? A certain pride, a certain awe, withheld him from offering to God even one prayer at night though he knew it was in God's power to take away his life while he slept and hurl his soul hellward ere he could beg for mercy; His pride in his own sin, his loveless awe of God, told him that his offense was too grievous to be atoned for in whole or in part by a false homage to the Allseeing and Allknowing.[1]

The retreat director, Father Arnall, unknowingly but effectively reinforces all this guilt, fear, and withdrawal. As one reads Joyce's presentation, one recognizes some of the words of the *Exercises* but not their heart or their consolation. That Stephen finds release in confession and in Communion does not symbolize the grace of the *Exercises* but the momentary resolution of psychic guilt. It is a brilliant portrait, one which allows us to begin our own reflections on the First Week of the *Exercises* by confronting some literary and, unfortunately, pastoral myths about the *Exercises* and the First Week:

1. The First Week of the *Exercises* is not about my own or anyone else's analyses of sin. It is about God's revelation about sinfulness.

2. God's revelation is always within a context of life and love; that is, God reveals what sin is so that I might be free from sin in order to live and to act out of love.

3. The great revelation of life and love is Jesus Christ who best teaches us what sin and forgiveness are about.

Then these three realities govern the *Exercises:* God's revelation to free us from sin that we may know life and love in Jesus Christ. This is the radical theological premise of the First Week of the *Spiritual Exercises.* What I propose to lay out here is: 1. An overview of the First Week, 2. The Centrality of Christ to the First Week, and 3. The relationship of the First Week and the Jesus this week presents to the subsequent three remaining weeks of the *Exercises.*

I. *An Overview of Week I*[2]

The First Week is both a structure and a movement. By "structure" I mean the planned external framework of the First Week of the *Exercises.* By "movement" I mean the planned internal dynamic or psycho-religious direction of the First Week of the *Exercises.* Consequently, "First Week" is an ambiguous term. It can designate time in the sense of chronological time; it can mean the framework of prayer forms and subject matter which makes up the Ignatian treatment of sin, mercy, forgiveness, and conversion; finally, it can mean the psycho-religious subjective process within the person who makes the *Exercises.*

The structure of the First Week is that of five presentations for five hours of prayer. The subject matter of those five hours is the revealed history of sin (specified in the sins of the angels, Adam and Eve, and an anonymous Christian), the personal history of sin in the life of the one who makes the exercises, and the consequences of sin unrepented, i.e, hell.

The individual meditations of the First Week have the following structure:

> 1. *Preludes:* These present the subject matter and particular graces sought. In the First Week the grace sought is that of "shame and confusion . . . because of the many . . . sins that I have committed," [48] or "a growing and intense sorrow and tears for my sins," [55] or "a deep sense of the pain which the lost suffer" [65].

> 2. *Points:* There are the distribution of the history to be prayed or the movement to be undergone, i.e., the parts which constitute the total experience of knowing what it is to be a loved and forgiven sinner.

> 3. *Colloquy:* This is the final, heart-to-heart conversation between the one making the retreat and the Lord, which represents the affective resolution of the Exercises.

By "affective resolution," I mean that St. Ignatius is less concerned about analyzing the components of sinfulness in human experience and rather intent with how the heart is touched by the personal reality of sin and forgiveness.

It is the movement of the *Exercises* which I want to emphasize, i.e, what are the psycho-religious affections towards which the *Exercises* lead? At this point let me spell this out. At the outset of the experience of the *Exercises,* Ignatius lays out what is expected of the director of this retreat. Among these twenty introductory reflections, the fifteenth is the most important. In this fifteenth annotation, or introductory remark, for the director, Ignatius says:

> The Director of the Exercises ought not to urge the exercitant more to poverty or any promise than to the contrary . . . Outside the *Exercises,* it is true, we may lawfully and meritoriously urge all . . . But while one is engaged in the Spiritual Exercises, it is more suitable and much better that the Creator and Lord in person communicate Himself to the devout soul . . . [15].

The movement of the First Week, then, is not a universal understanding of sin, forgiveness, and conversion. Rather the First Week invites personal understanding, and, therefore, a variety of understandings, about sin,

forgiveness, and conversion. For that reason, i.e., the personal quality of
sin, forgiveness, and conversion, Ignatius would invite the retreatant (the
one making the retreat) to find in the colloquies of the First Week the
one who alone resolves the mystery of sin—Jesus Christ. Note the sequence
of colloquies which are in the First Week.[3]

> Imagine Christ our Lord present before you upon the Cross . . . "What
> have I done for Christ?" "What am I doing for Christ?" "What ought I do
> for Christ?" [53]
>
> [G]iving thanks to Him . . . [61].
>
> The famous triple colloquy which asks first of Mary, then of Jesus, and,
> finally, of the Father three specific graces—knowledge and hatred of per-
> sonal sinfulness, a sense of their disorder and a desire for a reordering of
> one's life, and a knowledge of the world (see [63]).
>
> Enter into conversation with Christ our Lord . . . [71].

Thus the movement of the First Week of the *Exercises* is to see through
all the variousness of personal sinful actions a terrible sameness in the environment we have inherited, as a negative reality which we confirm in
our own lives, and whose reality is the dissolution of love. In God's light
all sin is radically a dehumanization, a taking away of life and of love. More-
over, for a Christian it has an added malice. In Christ, all creation has
been redeemed, restored to a relationship of friendship with the Father,
open again to the holiness of the Spirit, and once more capable of being
an environment of human union. For the Christian sin is a betrayal of the
restoration of friendship which Christ effected by his life, passion, death,
and resurrection.

In the triple colloquy of the third and fourth hours of prayer, suggested
in the First Week of the *Exercises*, the retreatant asks Mary, then Jesus,
and finally God the Father for three graces:

> an interior knowledge of one's own sinfulness and a hatred of this sinfulness;
>
> a sense of the disorder of one's life, i.e., what it is which causes this sinful-
> ness in me, and a new orientation towards order, i.e, a peaceful redirection
> of my life towards love;
>
> a knowledge of the world, i.e, as that reality which resists true life and love
> (not the world as the place where God can be found and served).[4]

The subjective and specific graces which Ignatius suggests in the First
Week are: to know my sins with heart-knowledge, to know with insight
their source, and to realize that nothing in creation can save me without
Christ. When a man or woman has such an enduring understanding of

the need for redemption, then Christ the Redeemer makes sense and becomes for that person, "My Lord."

In summary, then, we might say that the overall structure and movement of the First Week of the *Spiritual Exercises* is:

> A personal, prayerful encounter with one's need of a redeemer and the recurring assurance that the redeemer has been found, is available, and even now laboring in my life to bring me to the Father's Kingdom. That redeemer is Christ Crucified and Risen. It is Christ the Lord.

II. *Centrality of Christ in Week* I

Prayer is about our relatedness to God. The more intense the prayer, the more God dominates the prayer. As the First Week progresses, one of the signs of its authentic direction is the way that the retreatant begins to center on the reality of Christ as the one who saves and reveals to him or her what true life and love are.

Christ the Redeemer is the one who has encountered the enemy of the human and subdued him. The scriptural foundation of the First Week—for understanding the Christ available to the retreatant—is the Christ who encountered Satan's power and subdued it, who befriended sinners, and who led others to friendship with his Father. Let me spell this out.

In Mark's Gospel there are five key expositions of Christ's encounter with Satan (1:21-28; 5:1-20; 7:24-30; 9:14-29; and 3:22-27). In Mark the demonic is all that resists the establishment of the Kingdom of God to be effected through the ministry of Jesus.[5] For example, after the healing of the paralytic in Mark 2:1-12, there is a whole series of controversy stories, of Satan-inspired oppositions to the ministry of Jesus: "Why does he eat with such as these?" (Mark 2:16); "Why do John's disciples and those of the Pharisees fast, while yours do not?" (Mark 2:18); "Look! Why do they [the disciples] do a thing not permitted on the Sabbath? [the eating of grains of corn which they had plucked as they passed through a field] (Mark 2:24). The portrait of Jesus in Mark includes that of Christ who is a Great Exorcist, meeting Satan in Satan's tyranny over human beings, expelling Satan, restoring human wholeness, and doing this because he has come to plunder Satan's hold over the world (Mark 3:21-27).[6]

Not enough has been made of this important dimension of the *Exercises*. The theological setting of the First Week, in part, is the world without Jesus the Redeemer (the sins of the angels and the sin of Adam and Eve) or a world in which one acts as if Christ did not exist (the sin of the Christian who chooses non-Christ). This setting explains the first prelude of the First Week:

In a case where the subject matter is not visible, as here in a meditation on sin, the representation will be to see in imagination my soul as a prisoner in this corruptible body, and to consider my whole composite being as an exile here on earth, cast out to love among brute beasts. I said my whole composite being, body and soul. [47]

Note the parallel to Mark's Gospel account of Jesus' exorcism of the Gerasene demoniac:

> They came to Gerasene territory on the other side of the lake. As he got out of the boat, he was immediately met by a man from the tombs who had an unclean spirit. The man had taken refuge among the tombs; he could no longer be restrained even with a chain. In fact, he had frequently been secured with handcuffs and chains, but had pulled the chains apart and smashed the fetters. No one had proved strong enough to tame him. Uninterruptedly night and day, amid the tombs and on the hillsides, he screamed and gashed himself with stones (Mark 5:1-5).

What Ignatius invites the retreatant to experience is his or her radical need for Christ as Redeemer. Implicit in this is the realization that even baptized Christians can live—practically—as if Christ had not come.

The conversion of the First Week is not just from sin, as an obstruction, but to Christ as the foundation of a new creation, of a new worldview in which the retreatant comes to love him who gave his life for me [53]. The question that must arise is what kind of Redeemer is this? Is the Christ who conquered Satan a Redeemer who enslaves? tyrannizes by a moral haughtiness? In other words, does Christ supplant the power of Satan with another power? Yes—but it is the power of love. And another important Ignatian sensitivity is to make a colloquy of mercy [61]. That heart to heart conversation, the climax of the consideration of personal sins [55–61], would have no meaning if the retreatant were not also invited to recall how Christ treated sinners.

Let us return to Mark's narrative of the Gerasene demoniac. After the expulsion of "Legion," the townspeople "come to see what had happened"

> As they approached Jesus, they caught sight of the man who had been possessed by Legion sitting fully clothed and perfectly sane . . . (Mark 5:15).

To be saved by Jesus is not to substitute one tyranny for another but to become human again. It is so very important that the context, what I term the theological setting of the First Week, be reverenced by the director. "Sin" is not the subject matter of the First Week; redemption is. And it is important to see redemption as Jesus preached and donated it:

The tax collectors and sinners were all gathering around to hear him, at which the Pharisees and the scribes murmured, "This man welcomes sinners and eats with them" (Luke 15:1-2).

In answer, Jesus tells the great parables of Mercy—of the lost sheep (Luke 15:4-7), of the lost coin (Luke 15:8-10), and the Prodigal Son (Luke 15:11-32).

Finally, while the Kingdom reflection introduces the dedication of the Second Week, it is not absent from the First Week. To choose to be with Christ is to enter his Kingdom, to become a friend to the people of the Kingdom, symbolized in the great triple colloquy of the third [62–63] and fourth *Exercises* [64] of the First Week. To repent is, as Luke especially emphasizes, to make heaven-happy (Luke 15:7, 15:10, 15:32).[7]

The First Week centers on the conversion of the setting of, the creating of, the heart, that psycho-religious set of affections, values, and choices, whereby a retreatant wants to be saved by Christ in order to be fully human and part of Christ's Kingdom. The Second Week centers on how to labor in the Kingdom; the First Week on how to yearn for the freedom and peace of that Kingdom. Without Christ there is no First Week.

Consequently, there is no mercy meditation in the First Week because it is all mercy. There is no incompatibility in using the exorcism narrations, the parables of mercy, Christ's friendship with sinners, and his desire to lead us to his Kingdom as part of the First Week reflections. Again it is not a slavish literalism which makes a retreat "Ignatian," but a careful responsiveness to the graces of the *Exercises*, laid out in the preludes of petition and in the colloquies.[8] Indeed, it may well be that no one can really pray about his or her own sinfulness as Christian until that man or woman knows Christ's love for sinners.

III. *The Relationship of the First Week to the Rest of the* Exercises

The First Week establishes the radical process of the *Exercises*, i.e., the way the *Exercises* achieve their goal. That process is one of prayer and interpretative experience. By "interpretative experience" I mean the way the director helps the retreatant come to know the origin and direction of the various internal movements one will undergo in the *Exercises*, i.e., the discernment of spirits. Prayer and this interpretative experience are the foundations for knowledge, love, and service, the recurring petition in the Second Week.

The First Week also establishes the authority of personal encounter and developing relationship to God. In other words, it is the *caveat* voiced to the director in annotation #15: "But while one is engaged in the *Spirit-*

ual Exercises, it is more suitable and much better that the Creator and Lord in person communicate Himself to the devout soul . . ."[15] It is important for the retreatant to trust his/her experience, to believe that God can deal directly with him or her. Such confidence is not at all incompatible with a humble willingness to be helped to discern correctly. Indeed, the more one trusts God's goodness, the more one is willing to find every revelation of that goodness. And in the process of the *Exercises* God does give good things through the advice, support, and clarifications of the director.

The First Week introduces the retreatant to the method of discernment, an habitual awareness of what leads to life and love or what leads from life and love. It is the revelation that every human history and every human interior life has a pattern, a repetition of learned ways of assessing good and evil. The First Week conversion is, in large measure, a conversion towards assessing these acquired values against Christ's values. Discernment is not just judgment but judgment for the Kingdom.

Finally, the First Week radicalizes the retreatants affections in Christ as the revelation of who God is "for me." The First Week colloquies emphasize the personal concern Christ has that I be free from sin in order to be free for life, true life.

There are important dispositions in which the subsequent weeks of the *Exercises* will mature. Let me briefly relate how the subsequent weeks of the *Exercises* develop these dispositions, centering them always on the relationship between Christ and the retreatant.

The Second Week continues the process of deepening the personal relationship between Christ and the retreatant. It does this by centering on companionship, offering the retreatant the grace to accompany Christ on his work for the Kingdom. The discernment centers on how one will live for the Kingdom. It is a movement from redemption to discipleship.

The Third Week continues the theme of accompaniment with Christ, moving with him into the dark corridors of Christ's and all human suffering and death. It is a personal willingness to bear the cost of discipleship.

The Fourth Week further develops the theme accompaniment, moving into the empowerment of Christ's resurrection. This empowerment is one that leads to light and love. The Risen Jesus does not "get even" with his accusers or his betrayers or his executioners. Neither does the Risen Jesus recriminate his apostles for their cowardice and flight. His whole action is to restore, to renew trust, and to reestablish the community of the Kingdom. Thus the movement is from the cost of discipleship to the rewards of discipleship.

The First Week is important because in its graces depends the developed sense of discipleship which constitutes the kind of person who leaves the *Exercises.*

Conclusion

The First Week experience of the *Spiritual Exercises* is not as Joyce portrayed it—a relentless assault on the adolescent in all of us, terrifying us into confession. Neither is the First Week a moralizing set of sermons designed to get us to do what we already know we are supposed to do. Rather the First Week of the *Exercises* is a religious invitation to come to know and to love and to serve Christ the Redeemer by accepting our life in Him. It is the Ignatian belief that to know oneself as loved even in sin strengthens one to live in the likeness of that love; and, as the poet has suggested, to live in such love makes all the difference because

> In a flash, at a trumpet crash
> I am all at once what Christ is,   since he was what I am, and
> This Jack, joke, poor potsherd,   patch, matchwood, immortal
>   diamond,
> Is immortal diamond.[9]

NOTES

[1]James Joyce, *A Portrait of the Artist As A Young Man* (New York: The Viking Press, 1966) 103–104.

[2]There are several good, contemporary commentaries on the First Week. I want to cite some I have found most helpful and which have helped me formulate my own interpretation: Charles A. Bernard, S.J. *Elements pour un Directoire des Exercises,* Rome: Centrum Ignatianum Spiritualitatis, 1978) 40–48; Coathalem, Herve, S.J., *Ignatian Insights, a Guide to the Complete Spiritual Exercises,* Trans. Charles J. McCarthy (Taichung, Taiwan: Kuang Chi Press, 1961) 99–129; Winoc De Broucker, S.J., "The First Week of the Exercises," *Christus,* 21 (1959) 22–39; Marc Hoel, "Conversion and Solidarities: the First Week and the Kingdom," in *The Exercises and the Collective Dimension of Human Existence, Centrum Ignatianum Spiritualitatis* Series, 1979, 35–54; *The Way Supplement* for August 1983, vol 48 is on "Presenting the First Week"; cf. especially, Joseph Veale, "The First Week: Practical Questions," 15–27.

[3]On the Christ-centeredness of these colloquies see Hugo Rahner, *Ignatius the Theologian,* trans. Michael Barry (New York: Herder and Herder, 1968) 59–93.

[4]See [63].

[5]See G. R. Beasley-Murray, *Jesus and the Kingdom of God* (Grand Rapids: Eerdmans, 1986) 85–89.

[6]See G. Lohfink, "Die Korrelation von Reich Gottes und Volk Gottes bei Jesus," *THQ* 165 (1985) 173.

[7]See Joseph A. Grassi, *God Makes Me Laugh, a New Approach to Luke* (Wilmington: Michael Glazier, 1986) 123–131.

[8]See Veale, "The First Week," 20; also John Coventry, "Sixteenth and Twentieth Century Theologies of Sin: Can We Still Give the Text as it Stands?," *The Way Supplement* 48 (1983) 50–59.

[9]Gerard Manley Hopkins, "That Nature is a Heraclitean Fire," in the *Poems of Gerard Manley Hopkins,* eds. W. J. Gardner and N. H. Mackenzie, 4th ed. (New York: Oxford University Press, 1967).

5

The Kingdom and the Two Standards: Some Issues and Reflections

Kenneth J. Galbraith, S.J.

With Kenneth Galbraith's presentation, we come directly to the dynamics of the Second Week of the Exercises *and indeed to the heart of their articulation of Ignatius' inspiration. The meditations on the Kingdom and the Two Standards are not only those that most frequently come to mind at the mention of the* Spiritual Exercises *of St. Ignatius, but they are also often the most misunderstood and, in today's changed cultural situation, the most controverted. Galbraith offers remarkable insights that go a long way to resolving such controversies. While discussing the medieval imagery of the lord-vassal relationship that lies behind the meditation on the Kingdom, and the problems contemporary exercitants have concerning the image of a king, of total commitment, and the excessively male and military images of this meditation, he shows how the first part of that meditation allows us to create with God's approval an ideal or a "transcendent self" in our following of Christ. The male-dominated imagery is then illuminated with the help of insights from Jung and the military images are made more understandable in view of the interior and exterior struggle that work for the Kingdom entails. Similarly, the symbol of self-effacement or humiliation in the meditation on the Two Standards is translated in terms of truthful self-definition.*

I want to begin this presentation by quoting from the work of a man on fire with a vision. The man is the prophet Isaiah. The vision is how he conceived God's work with His people:

On this mountain the Lord of hosts will provide for all peoples
A feast of rich food and choice wines,
juicy, rich food and pure, choice wines.

The Lord God will wipe away the tears from all faces;
The reproach of his people he will remove
from the whole earth;
for the Lord has spoken.

On that day it will be said: "Behold our God, to whom we looked to save us!
This is the Lord for whom we looked; let us rejoice and be glad that he
has saved us!"
For the hand of the Lord will rest on this mountain
(Isa 25:6, 8-10).

When I read this passage as the first reading in the liturgy of the twenty-eighth Sunday in Ordinary Time, I had the subject of this lecture in my mind. I quickly flashed from Isaiah to another man of mystical vision who followed Isaiah by some two thousand years and who spoke his vision in what we know today as the *Spiritual Exercises*. The man, of course, is Ignatius Loyola, a Basque, a pilgrim, former soldier and courtier, who, following a profound religious conversion, became enraptured with the thought of serving another kind of king, his sovereign Lord and Savior.

The passion of Isaiah and Ignatius are the same. Yet a difference lies in their vision. Isaiah appears to picture a God who will create on his own a promised land for his people. Ignatius, on the other hand, does not see God doing something apart from us, as Isaiah seems to suggest, but offers us instead a vision of God inviting us into the work itself, offering us a part in the realization of the vision. Dedicated to the service of a divine King whose appointed task is to bring about the reign of God on earth, we share in the suffering and the toil of bringing it all about and ultimately partake, too, in the joy of the dream realized. We are sharers in the enterprise, not merely the beneficiaries of an inheritance created for us.

The Kingdom Meditation and Its Imagery

The vision Ignatius creates for us is found in his *Spiritual Exercises* at the beginning of the Second Week and is entitled the Call of the Temporal King. Ignatius proposes his vision in this manner:

There are two unequal parts in this consideration, the first one naturally leading to the more important second part.

1. In the first part, let me put myself into a mythical situation—the kind of story-truth of which fairy tales are made. I imagine a human leader, selected and raised up by God our Lord himself; every man, woman, and

child of good will is drawn to listen to such a leader and is inspired to follow his call.

His address to all rings out in words like these: "I want to overcome all diseases, all poverty, all ignorance, all oppression and slavery—in short, all enemies of mankind. Whoever wishes to join me in this undertaking must be content with the same food, drink, clothing, and so on, as mine. So, too, he must work with me by day, and watch with me by night, that as he has had a share in the toil with me, afterwards he may share in the victory with me." If a leader so attractive and inspiring and so much a man of God makes such a call, what kind of a person could refuse such an invitation? How could anyone not want to be a part of so challenging and noble an adventure?

2. In the second part, I consider Jesus Christ our Lord and his call. If a human leader can have such an appeal to us, how much greater is the attraction of the God-Man, Jesus Christ, our Leader and King! His call goes out to the whole of mankind, yet he specially calls each person in a particular way. He makes the appeal: "It is my will to win over the whole world, to conquer sin, hatred, and death—all the enemies between mankind and God. Whoever wishes to join me in this mission must be willing to labor with me, so that by following me in suffering, he may follow me in glory."

With God inviting and with victory assured, how can anyone of right mind not give himself over to Jesus and his work? (F 65, 67 cf. [91ff.]).

Ignatius places this meditation on the call of the gracious King at the very beginning of the Second Week of the *Exercises*. The retreatant, having passed through the first portion of the *Exercises*, stands full in the consciousness of his or her relationship with God, aware of God's faithful and constant love toward the retreatant and toward the world, despite any history of unloving behavior on the retreatant's part toward self, toward others, or toward the divine Majesty itself. God's merciful love, never fully understood, is nonetheless accepted in its richness and its personal direction toward the retreatant.

There is more yet to come. God will not be outdone. Love will find union by God becoming man, fully revealed in the person of Jesus. And not only will our humanity experience a new kind of dignity in God becoming incarnate, we will be shown in the person of Jesus and in his words what being truly human really means. He is Way, he is Truth, he is Life. Above all, he is the true servant of Yahweh, fully responsive to the divine Creator.

Love is to be served. Steeped in the medieval tradition of courtly love, Ignatius had within him a keen recognition of how love was to be answered according to the medieval norm. Romances abounded in Ignatius' day, and we know that in the process of his recovery from wounds suffered in the battle of Pamplona, romance novels were among the first things he requested.

But more significant than the tradition of courtly love was the lord/vassal tradition. It was born, of course, from necessity and in one form or another carried on through several centuries prior to Ignatius' time. It formed the basis of the entire medieval feudalistic system. Chaos and struggle marked the dark and middle ages in Europe. One could not rely on kinship to protect his lands and holdings from treachery, pillage, and invading enemies, but instead a ruler found advantage in receiving into his service those warriors who freely took service under a sovereign and fought with him and for him as a band of close comrades. The relationship, therefore, was highly personal. It emphasized friendship with the lord or chieftain, loyalty, bravery, mutual service, and above all, fidelity to the oath of fealty.

Mutuality characterized the bond between the lord and his servant or vassal. Each shared and each benefited through a kind of covenant of mutual dependency. In reward for service the vassal received from his lord certain benefices and a special rank in closeness. The vassal was not so much servant—despite the obvious hierarchical order—but a friend who enjoyed a special intimacy as adviser and companion. In the words of C. S. Lewis, it is important to note that

> the deepest of worldly emotions in this period is the love of man for man, the mutual love of warriors who die together fighting against odds, and the affection between vassal and lord. We shall never understand this last, if we think of it in the light of our moderated and impersonal loyalties.[1]

For his part, the lord received from his vassal service and respect, utter fidelity in all circumstances, unquestionable reliance in time of need, love, and a willingness to reach to the heroic if need should dictate. Nor were each bound to one another only in time of crisis or need. They were to share rest, enjoyment, abundance and peace together as well. In its ideal— and we must see it herein as just that—service on the part of the vassal was to be service in everything. On the part of the lord, his generosity and protection toward his vassal extended to every necessary dimension. Most of all, he was to attract the devotion of his vassal purely out of the richness and the goodness of his own character. The loyalty and the service of his vassals were to be in response to the lovableness and strength of character his vassals found in him.

In his monograph entitled "The Christ Experience and Relationship Fostered in the *Spiritual Exercises* of St. Ignatius of Loyola," Robert Schmitt remarks:

> With the growth of the ideal of the lord-vassal relationship there developed a corresponding ethical system, the picture of an ideal man with specific

virtues. Since the whole raison d'etre of the relationship was the development of reliable bonds, the most praised virtue became that of fidelity [in
love]. The entire structure of the ideal nourished a certain "mystique" of
service and fidelity that involved a commitment to serve one's lord at any
price.[2]

It is in terms of this cultural ideal that Ignatius found himself inspired
to fashion the person of Christ into the ideal king, himself a vassal, thereby
giving not only a new meaning to the significance of the cultural ideal but
also sparking within himself a motivating power for surrendering himself
to everything the transforming love of God might beget in him. For in
the king/vassal tradition, it was the attractiveness of the royal person, his
embodiment of every human virtue, that was to be the precise base for
winning the service of the vassal. It was the power of this embodiment
that would beget the undying loyalty of the vassal himself. Moreover, the
vassal recognized that everything embodied in the person of the king would
be directed in full toward the one invited to service. Consequently, the
mere knowledge of such an opportunity should move the heart of any
worthy knight to full generosity and service to the ultimate.

The Kingdom and My Transcendent Self

Or does it? Unfortunately, the desired response proposed in the meditation on the Call of the King is not always the response evoked in a modern day retreatant. All too often, the consideration becomes a real stumbling
block for reasons that are only too obvious. Basically, I see three:

1) Our inability to identify with the idea of king, however ideal we are told
the temporal king is;
2) The notion of total commitment to service in a cultural age wherein our
life experience has offered too few models that can reassure us that our generous response will be met with constancy and fidelity from the other side
in the form of protection, nurture, even support.
3) The excruciatingly male and militaristic imagery contained in the meditation.

This last point has a particular impact on women. Certainly, they are
as welcoming to the idea of challenge as any man is. And loving service
bears a strong appeal for them. Sharing in the foundation of a kingdom,
however, has little or no appeal. Nor do words like oppression, slavery,
enemy, struggle, conquer, and victory. Such words are allied with war and
war is killing and killing is totally foreign to the spirit of woman, who, deep
within her own soul recognizes herself as essentially a bearer and nurturer of life. In fact, we can safely say that, without an understanding and

careful approach to this portion of the *Exercises*, real damage could be inflicted on both the sexuality and the spirituality of men as well as women.

However, I would like to present here some reflections on the exercise of the Call of the King, hoping in doing so, not only to offset the above mentioned difficulties but at the same time to allow us to move to a fuller understanding of what is contained within the meditation itself.

First, the place where the retreatant finds himself or herself at the beginning of the Second Week is important for understanding what the meditation desires. The retreatant has a need. At the end of the First Week he or she is filled with a new consciousness, perhaps even a sense of awe and wonder, not only for the sense of God's merciful and provident caring in the face of life choices so inimical to one's well being, but also for God's loving fidelity toward a world bent on evil. The result, naturally, is a deep sense of gratitude. And gratitude likes to express itself. Hence, the grateful person genuinely wants *to do* something, wants to respond concretely in full expression of what the grateful person *feels.*

Enter the meditation on the Call of the King. It meets that need precisely. In its imaginative form, it offers to the retreatant a proposal that directs all the new found spiritual energy toward full expression of both desire and movement and at the same time provides something even more important: an opportunity for a deeper union with the incarnate, loving God.

The meditation, however, does something even more significant. The awareness of the first week centers on our dependency on God and what we as humans have done with that dependency, i.e., humankind's choice for non-life and the spiritual death that follows. Now a new insight is offered: I am not only loved, *I am needed.* God now chooses to be dependent on *me.*

Next, let us keep in mind the importance of the *imaginative* element that marks the meditation. In its first part, Ignatius invites us to picture "a human king chosen by God our Lord whom all Christian princes and men reverence and obey." This is not a Saul or a David or any other figure of history. Instead it is a leader, a human person, personally selected by God for the qualities he possesses for inspiring the reverence and the service of every human being. Yet because the king belongs to my imagination, I am free to imagine him as possessing every human quality that I as the retreatant would need in anyone who could win my heart and inspire my complete devotion, whether I as retreatant am a woman or a man. To state it in a slightly different way, Ignatius offers me the opportunity to imaginatively design my own king. This leader fashioned by me is also the one selected by God himself. In other words, *my ideal* has the divine stamp of approval.

Springing from my imagination and attracting all my energies because I myself have fashioned him as ideal, this imaginative leader is ultimately nothing more than *my transcendent self*: a reflection of everything I want to be as a full, human person. And because God would not choose as the fulfillment of the human heart a person who would not reflect all that God himself is, I can come to appreciate in a wholly new way that my transcendent self images the divine; that in moving to live out that which my imagination and heart have shown me what I am moving to become, I am reaching to the divine within me. That is what it means to love oneself.

Does this figure need to be imaged as king? Certainly not, if the image is in any way an obstacle to the meditation exercise itself. On the other hand, it is important that we recognize the significance of the *hierarchical* element. In other words, the figure that is to move me is greater in every respect than the person I presently find myself. What I see as present in him is what I want to integrate within myself. And because that which will move me as a human being more than anything else is love, the person I fashion in the meditation represents all the qualities I wish to find in the ideal loving person. It is the ideal leader's lovableness that is intended in the meditation on the Call of the King to attract my devotion and my full willing response. It is in this love, now seen as personally directed toward me that I wish to share. In such company I can only become more fully myself because the figure of the king, though greater than I in what he possesses, is really my transcendent self.

One more point on this notion of king. In the meditation the figure is king by reason of having been chosen by God the Creator. But he is ruler or leader, not merely by divine appointment from without, but, more important, for what he possesses within. More a figure of authenticity than of authority. In other words, it is what he possesses within himself, in the fundament of his own character, that gives him his position within the realm of all humanity. As archetypal king, he is the life principle of the realm, its libido, as well as the living principle of generativity, fertility, creativity in all the members of the kingdom.

Far from being a figure of power that dominates others, the true king is a source of life for others. He thrives when others thrive. He fosters creativity in others and rejoices when his subordinates prosper. He dispenses freely, blessing in a thousand ways with the richness of his person. In the words of Robert Moore, "he is the joyous archetypal parent who can bless."[3] He is potent, nurturing, engendering, and empowering. To be around him is to be better for the giftedness of his person which he so readily shares.

The king stewards and husbands the realm rather than governs it in the sense we know "govern." He creates order, not by coercing order, but by being ordered rightly himself. He can be center to the realm because he himself is centered. He fosters justice because he himself is just within and to know him is to know justice. In a word, his realm is the realm of human hearts and he forms the center and inspiration of that realm for the fullness of humanity he himself possesses. In him our sexuality can only thrive.

The Masculine and the Military

What can be said then about the notion of the masculine as found in the meditation? Is stressing the masculine so necessary, especially in the case of retreatants who have not had in their experience good male modeling? More important than the masculine element is the importance of recognizing that the ideal king is the king who is the center of all hearts. He can merit this position only if he possesses within him a character that is truly androgynous. As the ideal king, he is the archetypal man, integrated and whole. The integrated and whole male will embrace and express to the fullest the androgynous. This will be especially true when considering the figure of Christ as fully king but truly the androgynous male, too.

Carl Jung ascribed to Christ the term *conjunctio oppositorum*, the fusion of all opposites, the full spectrum of everything human and divine. If he was the source of life, he also knew death. With the power to miraculously feed others, he knew hunger. If he could show in himself the power to face even the most bitter of enemies and vanquish them, he also could be fully present to others as tender, caring, nurturing, and protective. Needed so much by others, he needed others himself. This was one who could turn humble, backward men into apostles who would bring the good news to every part of the known world, filled with a spirit that seemed to know no bounds. This was also one who could draw the devoted love of women who would stand by him in his darkest moment, drawn ever so deeply by the love they witnessed in him, love that directed itself so fully to each of them. This Jesus was a man's man, a woman's beloved. The Christ is humanity, male and female, ever moving to wholeness and unity-in-difference.

Lastly, what is to be done about the heavy stress Ignatius places on military metaphor, especially in light of what we said earlier? The problem of language might be resolved in recognizing that the true goal of the Christ is the establishment of a kingdom, "an eternal and universal kingdom, a kingdom of truth and life, a kingdom of holiness and grace, a kingdom of justice, love, and peace" (Preface of the feast of Christ the King). No kingdom, however, is a happenstance. It comes about with conscious effort and with struggle against all the forces that would oppose its existence. If it is a kingdom of love, and the kingdom of God is, then that kingdom will meet all the energy non-love can muster and a struggle is bound to ensue.

Moreover, despite the meditation describing the kingdom as being in the world, we need to remind ourselves of Jesus' words that "the kingdom of God is within you."[4] So it is that no matter how love is to be expressed in creating a more humane society about us, no matter how we view the world in the eyes of God as Ignatius will soon invite us to do in the coming meditation on the incarnation in the Second Week, we must first meet forces of non-love and non-life within ourselves. The reach for the transcendent self means an encounter with all dimensions of the self. And that spells struggle, no matter what metaphors are used to describe it.

The spiritual journey is the journey into the twofold mystery of God and of myself. The kingdom is both outside me and within me, for as humans we are essentially relational to others and to ourselves. The call of the King, therefore, is not just to a better world. It is an invitation to reach the full spiritual potential God originally created for me. The dream of the leader we envision in the meditation on the Call of the King is the dream of one who desires that fullness for every human being, knowing full well at the same time that the dream must necessarily be an ongoing process of transformation, not a goal. Into that process he committed himself wholeheartedly. As king, champion, magus, lover, nurturer, enabler, he personally invites each one of us to share in his journey because his journey is our journey and our journey is his. He has personally chosen to have it that way.

The Two Standards

In the flush of enthusiasm and early commitment made in the colloquy following the meditation on the Call of the King, the retreatant is ready for the task. All, however, is not easy, for the enemy is soon at work. Ignatius, understanding the significance of struggle, introduces us midway in the Second Week to another imaginative consideration aimed precisely toward our understanding that our best intentions in embracing the kingdom will meet forces inimical to our goal. He entitles the meditation "The Two Standards" or, as David Fleming in his popular version of the *Exercises* entitles it, "Two Leaders, Two Strategies" (F 85).

Time does not allow for going into the Two Standards meditation here in great detail, which is unfortunate because it truly forms an important element in the *Exercises* never really to be overlooked by one who is making them or directing them. For the sake of brevity, however, let us simply recall how Ignatius would have us imaginatively pose two leaders, each vying to hold sway in the world by having full power over every person's spirit. Both dispatch emissaries to do their work. The first is Satan, symbol of everything evil—that is, death to the spirit—who seeks his end by inviting one to riches and to honors and ultimately pride, seen as the ultimate rejection of the kingdom. The second, of course, is the person of Christ, who, standing for everything counter to death, advocates life to the fullest, first, through the embrace of spiritual poverty; secondly, by a willingness to risk rejection for not defining ourselves by worldly values; and thirdly by genuine humility.

The goal of the exercise, of course, is not a life choice to be made in favor of one leader or another. Early in the Second Week we have already made a fundamental option in favor of following God's chosen. Rather, if we are to look for the *raison d'etre* of the meditation, I believe it can be found within the third prelude of the exercise wherein Ignatius invites us to ask for the grace that we need, in this instance "the gift of being able to recognize the deceits of Satan and for the help to guard myself against them; and also . . . for a knowledge of the true life exemplified in Jesus Christ, my Lord and my God, and the grace to live my life in his way" (F 85 & 87).

The goal, then, is discernment, not choice. It is enlightenment to the subtleties that thwart the growth process and hinder the fundamental option for the full life. In other words, Ignatius recognizes that we are all prone to making choices that, far from begetting life within us, lead us to frustrate it. He recognizes that every choice we make in life whether it is as large and significant as life career or as apparently insignificant as looking at the values on which we build our personal relationships lead us either to become more who we are as persons or to regress. The former will make for one more step toward spiritual transformation, transcendence, new becoming; the latter will form one more option for stagnation, even regression as a person. The life force within us will be either enhanced or debilitated.

For example, out of respect for myself and for another it might be important that I make my anger known to the other person. We both are more alive for my doing so. On the other hand, my anger might have at its core the desire to destroy. I might justify my behavior on the basis that "he's had it coming for a long time." Deep inside me, perhaps, lingers unrecognized all the past hurts or rejections I failed to resolve, which emerge in the guise of my wrath over some single issue. The result is something destructive. And destructive behavior can hardly be life-giving.

What is essential, of course, is that I know the difference between what is life-giving and what is life-taking. Thus the need for the grace of discernment and the desire to exercise it because, whether it leads to fuller life or away from it, what lies before me always appears as *good and worthy*. In themselves there is nothing evil about riches, whether it be monetary gain or personal talent. Similarly, recognition of our person by others can have a genuine value for us. On the other hand, there is nothing basically good to be found in poverty, spiritual or actual, still less in being held in contempt or rejection. The latter, in fact, has played a destructive factor in the self-esteem of all of us and has led us all in different degree to withdraw from life rather than embrace it in its fullness. In other words, the emptiness and rejection we have known in our lives have only convinced us just how unlovable we really are. Praying for that hardly spells a recipe for becoming radically, spiritually alive.

Addressing the foregoing poses the need for us to look at what really constitutes pride on the one hand and humility on the other, for the Ignatian meditation definitely holds that in pride and humility lies the difference whether or not we reach for life or for its opposite.

I believe the key lies in how we choose to define ourselves. Pride, for example, is usually understood as an inordinate love of our own excellence. This inordinate element within pride lies not so much in relishing a quality or a giftedness in ourselves that seeks recognition—because that can even reflect God's glory—but in the idea that the inordinate leads us to define ourselves so narrowly as to deny that we are anything else but what we pride ourselves in, which is tantamount, of course, to living out an untruth. Its necessary consequence is detachment, alienation, and distancing myself from looking at the real truth of self and, for that matter, at God who is the source of my truth. It is as though I am what I define myself to be in my pride and nothing more.

Nor in my state of pride do I wish to recognize that I need to be more. In fact, I will even become defensive in maintaining the interior place in which I choose to define myself, whether it is as the best or, for that matter, even the worst. Harry Abbot Williams in his essay "Theology and Self Awareness" offers an example of a man who inordinately defines himself in terms of his intelligence.

> A man, for instance, may equate himself with his academic intelligence and ignore the rest of what he is. Such intelligence can cope with certain things in life. With regard to many other things, it is powerless. But the man thinks it can cope with everything. He ascribes to it an undue excellence and thus artificializes it. He makes of something real in its own sphere, something unreal by extending it beyond that sphere. He trusts his academic intelligence to establish and maintain a satisfying relation with his wife and children. This it cannot do. Thus he feels disillusioned and let down. He thinks it is the fault of others, when in fact it is the result of his own pride, the concentration of his faith upon one single aspect of himself, which shows

he is in a state of non-faith with regard to the rest of what he is—a condition which springs from his unbelief in God who creates and sustains his total being.[5]

The example speaks of a pride that emerges from a sense of excellence. However, lest we think that pride afflicts only those who excel, let us remember that there are some people who choose to define themselves even by their *affliction*, so that there is no one who has suffered more or who has been shamed more or who is on a lower rung on the ladder of self-esteem than they. These, too, cannot be touched nor will they reach to become something more, even though something more they really are. The result is total detachment from their true selves and from those around them, including the creative love of God.

Humility, on the other hand, has certainly little to offer as an antidote to pride if we take it in its usual connotation as a quality that merely advocates lowliness and self-effacement. The person who pursues self-effacement also pursues denial of self and untruth, thereby once again compromising movement within that person toward becoming more than conscious awareness says he or she really is.

However, humility in the true spiritual sense has less to do with viewing ourselves as lowly than with seeking to bring into our full consciousness the truth of who we really are. When, for example, the Virgin Mary gave recognition to her peasant status while she affirmed at the same time that her life had been touched by God and some day all the world would bless her, she spoke the truth of herself in all humility. And when Jesus said to his disciples, "You call me 'teacher' and 'master,' and rightly so, for indeed I am," (John 13:13), he, too, spoke from the same place.

The invitation in the meditation on the Two Standards, therefore, is the invitation to fullness of life by embracing the complete and utter truth of who we are. To choose otherwise is to move away from the standard of Christ and plant one foot firmly in the camp of Satan.

The truth of who I am, however, is never fully in my consciousness. It is a truth that unfolds only in time and comes to light only with great effort, the same as it did in the person of Jesus. As Elizabeth Boyden Howes in her book *Jesus' Answer to God* states it, Jesus' descent into the waters at the time of his baptism in the Jordan symbolized his coming forward

> . . . with all he knew of himself. It meant a confrontation with his own dark reality and the willingness to risk change by responding to the powerful cleansing meaning of water, producing opposing movements: the descent and the ascent.[6]

Yet all was not accomplished by one single gesture at the River Jordan. Jesus followed his baptism experience with a sojourn in the desert where he came to grips with the dark side of himself—imagined by the Synoptic writers as the figure of Satan tempting—which, if chosen, might have frustrated all that his God had called him to be.

In summary, the meditation on the Two Standards is simply another way of answering the question, "What is your addiction?" Addictions, being those dependencies we fear we cannot live without, are the subtle entrapments that forbid us from coming into knowing and accepting our whole self, darkness and light. Because we prize our addictions we value them as riches that will surely sustain us in everything we do. Unfortunately, we choose to define ourselves in them. "I can be this and nothing more." And the cycle of riches, narrow self-definition, and loss of true personhood follow. We frustrate our option for life.

I must end. But I do so in the hope that I have shown the Call of the King and the Two Standards as companion meditations having a single basic theme. The person of Christ is central to both. He is way and truth. In him lies our source of life. In us lies the choice to accept the life-giver and the gift in full.

NOTES

[1]C. S. Lewis, *The Allegory of Love: A Study in Medieval Tradition* (London: Oxford University Press, 1936) 9.

[2]*Studies in the Spirituality of Jesuits,* vol 6, no 5 (October 1974) 225–26.

[3]The citation is from "Rediscovering Masculine Potentials," a series of lectures delivered at the C. G. Jung Institute, Chicago, 1986. The description of the archetypal king contained in this essay is based on these lectures.

[4]See Luke 17:21. This traditional translation is, of course, disputed. See any current translation of this verse, e.g., the New American Bible's "The reign of God is already in your midst." The more recent exegesis of this verse, however, does not contradict and perhaps even supports the point being made [Editor's note].

[5]Harry Abbot Williams, "Theology and Self Awareness," in *Soundings: Essays Concerning Christian Understanding,* ed. A. R. Vidler (Cambridge: Cambridge University Press, 1966) 85.

[6]Elizabeth Boyden Howes, *Jesus' Answer to God* (San Francisco: Guild for Psychological Studies, 1984) 14.

6

Discernment in the *Spiritual Exercises*

Jules Toner, S.J.

For structuring the diverse viewpoints articulated in the multitude of books and articles that have been published in recent years on "discernment," it is good to have a clear presentation of the essentials of this important aspect of the Spiritual Exercises. *Jules Toner's lecture aptly fills this need. Through a careful analysis of the text itself, he clearly outlines Ignatius' teaching and shows the importance of distinguishing between discernment of spirits and discernment of God's will.*

There are many kinds of discernment which are needed in Christian life. There is, for example, discernment of true and false prophets and prophecies, discernment of true and false disciples of Christ, discernment of the signs of the times, discernment of genuine and spurious mystical experience, discernment of morally good and evil actions, discernment of spirits, discernment of God's will when no alternative in the concrete object for free choice is forbidden or commanded by any general, material moral principle.

The two latter forms of discernment are the ones on which St. Ignatius offers practical instruction in his *Spiritual Exercises*. Discernment of spirits is treated in what Ignatius calls "Rules for the Discernment of Spirits" [313–336]. Discernment of God's will is taken up where he gives directions on making "a sound and trustworthy election" [169–189]. It should be noted that, while Ignatius does use the phrase "discernment of spirits," he does not use "discernment of God's will." He speaks of seeking God's will, finding God's will, and making an election. Nevertheless, our current phrase, "discernment of God's will," is roughly the equivalent of what he means by making an election and, for our present practical purposes, the terms can be used as synonyms.

Discernment of spirits and discernment of God's will do overlap with some of the other forms of discernment noted above and with each other, but they are distinct from the other forms and from each other. It is surprising how many people, even among those who are knowledgeable about the *Spiritual Exercises,* think that discernment of spirits and discernment of God's will are the same thing. It is true that discernment of spirits is necessary for two Ignatian ways of discerning God's will, but the third way is not dependent on discernment of spirits; and discernment of spirits can be usefully done at times when the discerner does not have any decision about God's will to make.

It is impossible within a few pages to offer any satisfactory exposition even of the fundamentals of Ignatian discernment of spirits or discernment of God's will, much less of both. All that can be done is to present some introductory notion of what these two kinds of discernment are about and indicate their roles in the *Exercises* and their more general usefulness in our daily Christian lives for growing spiritually and collaborating with Christ for the sake of God's kingdom.[1]

Discernment of Spirits

Since what is in Ignatius' teaching on discernment of spirits is needed for understanding his instructions on the modes of discerning God's will, it should be taken up first. At the beginning of his rules for discerning spirits, Ignatius gives us a highly compressed heading to explain what they are about and what their purpose is:

> Rules for [getting in touch with and] understanding to some extent the different movements produced in the soul and for recognizing those that are good to admit them, and those that are bad, to reject them [313].[2]

Meaning of "Spirits." Before drawing out what is in this explanatory heading, let us see what meaning is to be given the word "spirits." There can be no doubt that, for Ignatius, this word referred to the Holy Spirit and to created spirits, both the good ones, those who are commonly called angels, and the evil ones, those who are commonly called Satan and demons. In using Ignatius' rules, we can and should give the term "evil spirits" a broader meaning which, besides Satan and demons, includes the tendencies in our own psyches which spring from egoism and disordered sensuality and also from other individual human persons or society insofar as these are an influence for evil in our lives.

It is neither necessary nor possible in all instances to portion out the influence for evil among all these sources. We can, with some clarity and accuracy, become aware of our own bad habitual inclinations and of the bad influence of other human persons; and it is important to do so in order to eliminate, or at least control, the effect of such influences in our lives. How much an evil spirit may be at work along with these influences or when he is the primary instigator of an evil movement, are questions we cannot answer and do not need to.

Could it be that there really are no created evil spirits such as Ignatius believed in and that we can, in our day, eliminate them from consideration? Some would readily respond affirmatively and seem to assume that their opinion is common among theologically sophisticated Christians. For myself, I find grave problems with that assumption and with such an easy response. During about thirty years of teaching Ignatian discernment, mostly to highly educated, mature Christian women and men, experienced as teachers and leaders in the Church's life, I have not found more than a handful who had any doubt about the existence of created spirits, good or evil. Frequently, with groups or individuals, I have asked about their beliefs regarding such spirits in order to avoid talking at cross purposes with them and have found no more than one or two who disbelieved or had difficulty about believing in those spirits. In my reading of reputable theologians on this question, I have not come across any indication that the percentage of doubters is notably greater than it is among the people I have taught. The few who deny the existence of spirits seem to do so in order to be more in accord with contemporary modes of thought and seem to think that somehow or other (never made clear how) modern depth psychology or modern scriptural scholarship has made belief in good or evil created spirits theologically naive.

This is not the place to question the logic and even the theological criteria employed in their reasoning. The only purpose for bringing up the issue here is to say two things. First, no Christian believer needs to be embarrassed if he or she accepts as real the spirits which St. Ignatius speaks about as if he or she were a remnant of the dark ages. Second, anyone who does not accept the reality of such spirits can still accept the Ignatian rules for discernment of spirits while meaning by spirits the Holy Spirit and those elements given above in the broad meaning of evil spirit.

Meaning of "Different Movements." Returning to Ignatius' explanatory heading, what does he mean by "different movements"? These include cognitive acts (e.g., thoughts, fantasies, memories), affective acts (e.g., love, desire, hate, aversion, hope, fear), and affective feelings (e.g., lightheartedness, depression, gloominess, sweetness, bitterness)—in short, all that goes on in our minds and hearts. However, it is clear that Ignatius is not concerned about all these inner movements; his interest is limited to acts of faith, hope, and charity, the core of our Christian spiritual life, and then to whatever other movements tend of themselves to have an influence on faith, hope, and charity. What he calls good movements are those which of themselves tend to energize and build up one's life of Christian faith, hope, and charity; and, on the other hand, those which he calls evil are those which of themselves tend to weaken and ultimately to destroy that life.

It would be a serious mistake to think that, in these rules, Ignatius is principally concerned with unusual, even sensational, spiritual experiences. The rules do help in dealing with these experiences, but what Ignatius is mainly concerned about is to help us understand and respond wisely to the ordinary spiritual or anti-spiritual movements of everyday Christian life.

It would also be a serious and very harmful mistake to think that these movements by themselves make us better or worse Christian persons. The movements Ignatius is concerned about are merely spontaneous ones, which arise prior to any free and responsible act. I am not, St. Ignatius says in one of his letters, a better person because of the good movements I experience nor worse because of the evil ones. It all depends on how I, with my freedom, respond to these movements, freely accepting them and acting on them or freely rejecting and expelling them, refusing to let them influence my actions. A good movement, e.g., an inclination to act generously or a feeling of joy in God, can be resisted or misused and result in spiritual harm; a bad movement, e.g., an inclination to selfishness or distrust of God, a feeling of aridity, can be the occasion for courageous resistance and for spiritual growth.

Threefold Purpose of the Rules. With the foregoing clarifications in mind, we can understand Ignatius' threefold purpose for the rules expressed in the explanatory heading. The first purpose is to help us get in touch with the diverse movements in us. We are in touch with these movements when we have a reflective and discriminating awareness of them, an awareness that is not easily or commonly achieved in any large measure. For most people, what goes on in consciousness is largely, in a phrase from William James, "a booming, buzzing, confusion." The first purpose is subordinate to the second, to understand the movements with which we have gotten in touch, of which we have become reflectively and discriminatingly aware. To understand them, in this context, means principally two things: to see how they of themselves tend to influence our Christian lives of faith, hope, and charity, either positively or negatively; and to judge what is their source, that is, by what spirit they are prompted. Reaching this understanding of inner movements is discernment of spirits properly speaking, and the rules are for the sake of helping us "to some extent" to do this. Finally, both the first and second purposes are subordinate to a third, that of helping us to open ourselves to the influence of good movements and close out the evil ones. This is the ultimate purpose of the rules, to help us overcome the influence of the evil spirit and to allow the Holy Spirit to lead us to ever fuller union with God in Christ.

The Role of Discerning Spirits in the Spiritual Exercises. What has just been said about the subject matter and the threefold purpose of the rules makes it obvious how helpful they can be to anyone for living in union with Christ a life under the sway of the Holy Spirit. But they have a special role in the *Exercises.* For the *Spiritual Exercises,* in their most proper form, are made by an individual under the direction of someone who has a deep understanding of their dynamics. This director needs to be apprised of the significant spiritual movements going on in the directee and be able to understand them. Only so can he or she help the directee to be open to the Holy Spirit, to overcome the frontal attacks of the evil spirit, and to uncover his deceptions. Only so can the director make wise decisions about what spiritual exercises would, at any time during the *Exercises,* likely be most helpful for this individual directee. Further, as will appear in our next step, two of the three "times" at which Ignatius says we can make a trustworthy election are times at which God gives spiritual motions. To recognize and evaluate these experiences, the rules for discernment of spirits are of critical importance; without them, there would be grave danger of deception and illusion in discerning God's will.

Discernment of God's Will

The second form of spiritual discernment treated in the *Spiritual Exercises* of St. Ignatius is that of discerning God's will. To understand what this discernment is about, three things must be clear:

1. What the meaning of "God's will" is in this context;
2. What the requisite conditions for a sound and trustworthy discernment are; and
3. What Ignatius means by the three times for, and three modes of, such discernment.

Meaning of "God's Will." First, what is the meaning of the term "God's will" in the context of Ignatian discernment? In different contexts, the term can have many different meanings; and, unless the meaning in this context is carefully delimited, a great deal of nonsense could be mistakenly attributed to Ignatius.

God's will as object of Ignatian discernment is God's *positive*, as distinct from his merely permissive, will. God permits many things which he would not will positively, for example, sin and the consequences of sin.

Among the things that God wills positively, some he wills with an effective and necessitating will. Such things happen independently of our free choice; we can freely choose to accept them lovingly and trustingly or we can choose to respond rebelliously, but we have no choice about their happening or not happening. God's will in this meaning we can know only by prophecy or after the event. It is entirely outside the scope of Ignatian discernment. On the other hand, some things which God wills positively, he leaves to our free choice; concerning these, God has a preferential but non-necessitating will. We can try to find, and can freely choose to do or not to do, what God prefers. In these matters about which we have a free choice, Ignatius is not concerned with finding God's universal will, e.g., the principles of moral theology; he is concerned only with God's preferential will regarding the choice by an individual (or by a particular group) in some concrete situation.

However, not every concrete situation about which God has a preferential will but leaves to the individual's free choice is within the compass of God's will as object of Ignatian discernment. Ignatius sees two different areas for discerning God's will regarding the individual's choices. In one of these, the person is trying to find out whether a proposed alternative for choice is morally commanded or forbidden. In the other area, he already judges that every alternative for this choice is neither forbidden nor commanded nor commended by God; and he is trying to discern which one is more for the glory of God. Ignatius' methods of discerning God's will are concerned solely with God's will in this latter area.

Essential Conditions for Sound Discernment of God's Will. If we are to have any justifiable hope of finding God's will in the circumscribed meaning just explained, two essential conditions must be fulfilled; if we are to have any justifiable confidence that our discernment has led us to what is God's will, we must be justifiably confident that we have fulfilled these conditions. They are based on several beliefs. The first is our belief about God: that God in his infinite wisdom knows which alternative in the concrete situation for choice is more for the glory he wants to communicate to us; that he has the power to lead us to a true judgment; and that, in his boundless love, he will do so if we freely open ourselves to let him lead us. The other beliefs are about our relationship with God in seeking and finding his will. One of these beliefs is that we are entirely dependent on God leading us in our discernment. No evidence which we can find for what is God's will, no matter how great our intelligence, experience, and effort can give more than some probability, never enough to justify a conviction that we have judged truly. Another belief is that when God leads us to a true judgment about his will, he ordinarily does so through the sincere and generous efforts of our own minds and hearts. His help will not substitute for our human efforts. He will guide our efforts; but without our efforts, there is nothing for him to guide.

From these beliefs flow the requisite conditions for sound and trustworthy discernment of God's will: in our discernment, we must be as open as we can be to the Holy Spirit; and we must make our utmost reasonable effort in searching for God's will.

Openness to the Holy Spirit in Christian life in general is fundamentally constituted by faith, hope, and charity, with the humility that is prerequisite to, and consequent on, these. Within the particular context of discerning God's will, certain particular expressions of faith, hope, and charity in a Christian life open to the Holy Spirit need to be stressed. The first is a sincere intention to do whatever God wills, no matter what the cost; to seek to find God's will with the intention of considering whether or not to do it once it is known is worse than a waste of time. A second element to be stressed is prayer of petition to know God's will, prayer of intense desire with faith that God will lead me to know it and with perseverance. The third element is indifference to every alternative for choice except insofar as it seems to be God's will. This element can be given other names, for example, detachment, freedom of spirit, purity of heart; but no name seems to bring out Ignatius' point as emphatically and clearly as does indifference to all but God's will.

Indifference, the common shorthand term for this third element in openness to the Holy Spirit is the hardest one to attain and the easiest to overlook. Therefore, it is the one which Ignatius, in his instructions on seeking God's will, never tires of recalling and emphasizing (See [1, 5, 16, 23, 146, 147, 155–157, 166, 169, 179, 184, 189]). It is the sure expression of, and test of, faith, hope, and charity, the ultimate criterion of openness to the Holy Spirit and, more than anything else, the key to successful discernment of God's will. All the meditation or contemplation and self-examination in the *Exercises* prior to the election is for the sake of achieving it. To understand it is fundamental for any understanding of Ignatian discernment of God's will.

The second essential condition for sound and trustworthy discernment of God's will, making our utmost reasonable effort, involves at least two things. It involves trying to learn the most secure and helpful methods of searching for God's will and learning how to use these methods by study, by experience of using them under direction, by reflection on our experience. It also involves, when carrying on a discernment, that we do so as diligently and as perseveringly as we reasonably can, giving it all the time and energy that is needed and reasonable in the actual situation.

Of the two essential conditions for a sound Ignatian election, the first one, openness to the Holy Spirit, seems to be far and away the more important—certainly for anyone who believes as firmly as Ignatius did in a lovingly provident God who "makes all things work together for the good of those who have been called" (Rom 8:28). Such a God will surely lead to what is for the greater glory those who are open to him in the ways described above even if, through no fault of their own, their best efforts to find his will are carried out in ways that lack practical wisdom about how to do it. Nevertheless, the second essential condition requires us to learn and to carry out the discernment process insofar as we have the ability and opportunity to do so.

Three Times for and Modes of Discerning God's Will. Now, whenever with human reason we try to reach a trustworthy practical decision, we have to get data and interpret the data in order to derive evidence for or against proposed alternative choices. Ignatius sees three kinds of data from which we can derive three kinds of evidence for what God wills in a concrete situation for choice. He gives ways of critically testing data when that is needed and offers appropriate principles for interpreting the different kinds of data so as to derive evidence. Two kinds of data are given by the Holy Spirit in spiritual experiences which, when understood and interpreted, serve as indicators of the direction in which the Holy Spirit is drawing the discerner. The third kind of data is gathered by rational investigation (by observation, remembering past experiences, research, etc.) of the facts about self and the concrete situation and by surmising the likely consequences of each alternative choice—consequences, in this kind of decision, for the greater or lesser service and glory of God.

Accordingly, Ignatius speaks of three "times" or opportune occasions at which one who has a decision to make can undertake a sound discernment of God's will [175–177]. The first two times or occasions occur when God actually gives the spiritual experiences which serve as data; the third time or occasion is present when the discerner is in tranquillity, that is to say, is neither having the spiritual movements of the first and second times nor is disturbed by anything that would hinder calm and clearheaded rational investigation.

Corresponding with each of these three times is a mode of seeking God's will. These are commonly called the first, second, and third modes of election, of discerning God's will, or the first-time, second-time, and third-time modes.

There is very much that needs to be said about each of these times for and modes of, discerning God's will if they are to be understood accurately and in a way that is helpful in practice. What is said in order to convey such understanding will be profoundly influenced by which of the conflicting interpretations of the Ignatian text one subscribes to. It is impossible within the limits of this essay to explain the three times and modes, much less to take account of the various interpretations that have been offered.

The Role of Discerning God's Will in the Spiritual Exercises. To fulfill my limited aim stated above as possible and intended, something should be said about the role within the *Spiritual Exercises* of Ignatius' teaching on discerning God's will. The very first paragraph in that document makes it evident that discerning God's will is central to its dynamics. There he says that the *Exercises* are "every way of preparing and disposing the soul to rid itself of all inordinate attachments, and, after their removal, of seeking and finding the will of God" [1]. The whole first half of the *Exercises* leads up to, prepares the exercitant for, the election by freeing her from inordinate desires and aversions and enabling her to love God and neighbor with such a pure and intense love as to be indifferent to all but God's greater glory in his sons and daughters and, consequently, be able to find God's will. The second half of the *Exercises* is to strengthen the exercitant in her resolve to carry out what is chosen as God's will.

Ignatius' instructions on the election in the *Spiritual Exercises* are clearly not meant exclusively for the time of the *Exercises.* They are to guide us, not only in making critically important decisions at other times, but also in making ordinary, even everyday decisions. For the core of Ignatian spirituality is concerned with striving to achieve a pure heart, a heart with one love for God and our neighbor in God, with one desire to live with Jesus for the kingdom of God, and so be able to find and do God's will at all times and in everything.

NOTES

[1]There is a variety of conflicting opinions on how to understand what Ignatius has written both on discernment of spirits and on discernment of God's will. I have presented in detail my interpretation of Ignatian teaching on discernment of spirits, some major opposing opinions, and my reasons for preferring mine in a book entitled, *A Commentary on St. Ignatius' Rules for the Discernment of Spirits* (St. Louis: The Institute of Jesuit Sources, 1982). A second volume has just appeared from the same publisher, *Discerning God's Will.* It does the same task for Ignatius' teaching on individual dis-

cernment of God's will. More directly practical guidance for discerning God's will can be found in a workshop handout entitled "Some Practical Helps for Individual and Group Discernment of God's Will." These pages can be obtained through Mrs. Teri Larocque, Colombiere Center, P.O. Box 139, Clarkston, MT 40106.

[2]Cf. the note on the translation of this title in Puhl, 193.

7

Praying the Passion:
The Dynamics of Dying with Christ

Peter J. Fennessy, S.J.

Once a discernment process of discovering God's will, at least tenta-tively, has been reached, confirmation of the decision(s) is had by encoun-tering the Lord in his passion and death (Third Week) and resurrection (Fourth Week). Peter Fennessy's offering provides a deeper psychological insight into "dying to self" in our attachments, fears, and desires, through contemplation of the suffering and death of Jesus. Indeed, it is doubtful that a more thorough contemporary correlation of the contemplation of the pas-sion of Christ with the psychological dynamics of the Exercises is available.

Introduction

Our topic is praying about the suffering and death of Jesus in the third week of the *Spiritual Exercises*. In the First Week we looked at sin and forgiveness, in the Second Week we looked at Christ and made a com-mitment to follow him, in the Third Week we contemplate his suffering and death. We shall look especially at some psychological mechanisms that are operative in the Third Week. Once we make a commitment, the fears we have of it and our desires for other things come back and try to change that commitment. These fears and desires are very closely related to suffer-ing because they caused our suffering in the past: we suffer meeting what we fear or losing what we desire. They have taught us what suffering is. And so these are the glasses through which we look at Christ's suffering. We will see him encountering what we fear and losing what we desire. We will approach his sufferings one at a time, selecting the one that we are ripe for at that particular moment. By staying with Christ, by our compassionate suffering with him, we will die psychically with him to what we fear and to what we desire; we will die to them one by one until we have died to all fear and all desire and have set aside everything that threatens our election. And then we will experience that this death to everything except Christ and God's will is not death at all; but that by letting go of our fears, we have fallen into the hands of God and that we have there everything, God and all that is his. And this experience of a life beyond suffering and death will also help us to face the sacrifices demanded by our election.

We will speak about what I call the psychological dynamics of the Third Week and the mechanisms that make up that dynamism. Grace is much more important than these psychological mechanisms, but the mechanisms are easier to analyze than grace is, and they are the elements of our own psychology, the secondary causes, through which grace usually operates. These mechanisms will be much more explicit than we ever encounter in making or directing a retreat, and that is so that we can more easily understand them. There may also be other ways of analyzing the experience of this week, but I am picking an extreme analysis, psychic death, because I think that kind of extreme can be used as a limit case against which to measure other analyses and experiences.

We should stress that this is just one explanation of the Third Week dynamic, it is not necessarily *the* explanation. There are other analyses of this week. There may even be several valid explanations—Ignatius warns us not to try to lead all souls in the same way.

A lot of reflective work needs to be done on this week. The dynamics of the four weeks are parts of one united whole. Entering the dynamic of the Third Week depends on having substantially completed the dynamic of the previous weeks. Hence we may say even *a priori* that each week is progressively less experienced than the previous one, and retreat directors will tell us, I believe, that this is borne out in reality, that there is less *de facto* experience of the Third Week. Consequently there is also less speculation and writing about it. I hope the following suggestions will stimulate further questions and discussion.

Prior to the Third Week

The suffering that may be our lot in the Third Week has already been hinted at prior to the election, hinted at in fact by most of the main meditations of the *Exercises:*

a. In the First Principle and Foundation [23] we are told that we must make ourselves indifferent to sickness, poverty, dishonor, and a short life.
b. In the Kingdom Meditation, the King invites us not just to friendship, but to suffering: to work and toil and watch by night with him [93], to labor with him and follow him in suffering [95]. Ignatius presents us with a prayer where we ask to imitate Christ in bearing all wrongs and all abuse and all poverty [98].
c. In the Meditation on the Two Standards we are invited to poverty, even actual poverty, and to a desire for insults and contempt [146].
d. In the Consideration on the Three Kinds of Humility we are invited to desire and choose poverty with Christ poor, insults with Christ loaded with insults, and to be deemed as worthless and foolish, because Christ was treated like this before us [167].

The Election

The *Spiritual Exercises* bring us to an election. It may be just an implicit choice to follow Christ more closely, or it may be a much more explicit choice that concretizes our commitment to Christ in some very specific way. But that choice, election, or commitment has prepared for and will entail suffering; it certainly calls upon us to give up the other choices and to let go of what is not compatible with what we have chosen. That exclusion of what is in some way desirable is at the root of the suffering implicit in every choice. The election is the beginning of a movement from thinking and discernment into action and an encounter with all the forces of resistance that is met with in the world of action. And out of that encounter will come pain.

Inordinate Affections

Our inordinate attachments, those that are not in accord with the will of God, are going to be a key to the suffering that we shall encounter as a result of our election. Suffering arises out of conflict, and if our election is made in accordance with the will of God, it is certain to conflict with everything that is not in accordance with God's will or that may not be in accord with God's will at some future time. So we will begin by looking at inordinate attachments, but eventually we must consider every attachment that might conflict with God's will and with our following of Christ, for each of these has the potential to draw us away from God and we must be prepared to die to these as well.

Ignatius has already referred to these attachments, and we have already noticed through the retreat that these attachments have been at work in us. In the title of the *Exercises* [21], where Ignatius explained the purpose of the *Exercises,* he indicated and presupposed that we have certain inordinate inclinations. That is why in the First Principle and Foundation [23] he suggests the necessity and difficulty ("we must") of making ourselves indifferent. Meditating on our personal sin [56–57], we recall our sins and in the Triple Colloquy we beg for a profound knowledge not just of our sin but of the underlying disorder [62], that can lead us away from God's will and into sin. That disorder is something that will cause us suffering as we seek to follow the Lord. We may also have increased our awareness of this disorder by the feelings of repugnance that Ignatius instructs us to pray against [157] and by a personal adaptation of the tactics of the enemy to our own lives in the Meditation on the Two Standards [142].

These disorders have been overcome to a certain extent. The *Exercises* have had as their aim a sufficient freedom from these inclinations to make a well ordered election. But we have not gotten rid of them totally; they come back now out of a kind of instinct for self-preservation. The election itself contributes to the recrudescence of these attachments. If firmly adhered to and lived by, the election threatens the survival and free reign of these attachments, and so they reassert themselves. We know the story of Jesus fasting for forty days in the desert. The evangelist says that at the end of that time he was hungry. I always thought that, yes, at the end of forty days I would be hungry too. But a different kind of hunger is meant. When we set aside food totally, there is an initial hunger, and then it dies down. We do not feel the hunger. But when the body begins to feed on vital tissue, when death is imminent, the body reacts, and an enormous hunger takes possession of the person. The body does not want to die and it cries out against death, and neither do our inordinate inclinations want to die. Once a person becomes settled on one course of action, the fears and desires that may conflict with this election return with a renewed appeal. They must be dealt with until a person becomes so totally and absolutely committed to the one choice that the alternatives are, at least for a while, effectively killed.

These fears and desires also revivify because we are concerned with suffering in the Third Week, and they are connected with suffering: we have learned about suffering through fear and desire. We are meditating on the passion, and we are being urged by Ignatius to call to mind the sorrows and labors of Christ from his birth right up to the mystery we are meditating on [206]. As we shall mention shortly, we discern sorrow and suffering through the mediation of the fears and desires that cause us sorrow and suffering. Thus meditating on suffering brings these other emotions to greater prominence in our psychic life during this week.

These attachments also revivify because they are related to the sins we recall in the sixth point of each Third Week meditation. Our sins have had their root and cause in our attachments. We have sinned in the past because we have desired too much the possession or enjoyment of some good, or because we have feared too much some loss. The attachments that revivify after the election are not some totally different set of character faults, what revivify are our same old weaknesses.

There are a variety of causes that are moving these inordinate attachments into focus in our psychic life. This is important. Because we have made an election, we really have to deal with these feelings and disorders. It is better that they come to our consciousness at this point rather than just lying in wait until after the retreat is over, until after we start putting our election into practice. We might say then that we did not realize what would be entailed, that we might have chosen differently if we had known. When we chose to follow Christ, we may unconsciously have left open the possibility of many other goals and desires. This can lead to compromise and eventually to a repudiation of our election. In the Third Week the Lord will show us what we may have to suffer and may have to die to. We will be enabled by compassion with Christ (literally "suffering with" Christ) to deal with these inordinate inclinations and to deepen our choice of Christ even though it may mean the loss of everything else. We will come to that anterior affective renunciation that is the perfection of Ignatian indifference and that is the characteristic of the third class of men and women who have affectively *(en affecto)* left all they desired [155]. So in the Third Week we continue the dynamic that stretches from the meditation on the First Principle through the considerations surrounding the Election, and this dynamic also brings us from our initial election into a total commitment to the Lord.

If we understand this correctly, there is a new meaning given to the words "confirmation" and "compassion." It has been said that the purpose of the Third Week is the confirmation of the election, and this is sometimes thought to mean that if I receive consolation during the Third Week, it is a sign that I have made the right election, and that if I do not, it means that maybe the election should be remade. Confirmation really has this meaning: *confirmare,* to strengthen. The election we made is strengthened by our contemplations on the sufferings of Christ which put to death in us the forces that would overturn the election. Compassion is not looked upon too kindly by the Official Directory of 1599;[1] it is thought to be a less than useful sentiment. The reality of the situation is that compassion is a deep love of Christ that unites us to him in his suffering and in doing so brings us to renounce our own selves, it brings us into a state out of which the Christian life is lived even more fully. It brings about a state that is much more useful in the long run and more valuable than the other virtues referred to by the writers of the Directory. It is a sharing in the mystery of the death and resurrection of Christ which deepens our love, our self-abnegation, and our commitment to follow the Lord.

Subjective Specification

As I have mentioned, these fears and desires also determine to some extent our own suffering. Buddha said simply: suffering arises from desire and fear. We have suffered because we had to encounter what we feared or had to face the loss of what we loved. This is true first of all in mental and emotional suffering, but even physical pain is made far worse by the psychological suffering that accompanies it.

Our understanding and perception of suffering have grown out of our personal experience of suffering, and so out of our fears and desires. We understand the suffering that we have experienced, or that we fear; we understand the pain in the loss of a good that we ourselves desire. It is out of our personal appreciation of suffering that we will know what suffering is, and that we will be able to recognize it in the lives of others.

Our personal experience then, our weakness and sin and suffering, will determine how we perceive the suffering of another, and even, in the Third Week, how we perceive the suffering of Christ. We each will see in the same contemplations of the *Exercises* what is most applicable to ourselves. In a complex history or text, we are naturally drawn to the one incident or the one phrase that has the most meaning for us; and in a single incident or phrase that is susceptible to different interpretations, we will focus on the interpretation that is most pertinent to our own situation.

Our perception then is not totally objective, and this is not a bad thing. It occasions a personal knowledge that penetrates and involves our affections, emotions, and wills in a way that purely objective knowledge could not. This subjective quality of our perception permits us intuitively to pick out of a complex situation elements that are most appropriate and pertinent to ourselves. The *Exercises* can thus be adapted to the individual in a way that the director and even the retreatant could not consciously effect.

Need for Specification

In the Third Week we need subjective specification and selection of material. Ignatius prepares for this to happen. He presents us with an abundance of material, gives us plenty of time to see the various aspects of this material. He leaves us free to select what we wish and then urges us to concentrate on a small number of points.

First, unlike the single events of most of the rest of the *Exercises*, the titles of the contemplations in the Third Week indicate a continual flow from one moment to another, e.g., "from the garden to the house of Annas inclusive" [208]. Each contemplation considers *los misterios,* the mysteries of that part of the passion. And so each contemplation provides several mysteries or incidents, more than enough material for one meditation. Each incident all by itself [209] could be used as material for a separate meditation.

Second, Ignatius insists that retreat directors present the various points briefly, not developing them at great length [2]. The intention is to prevent directors from pushing their own interpretations and emphases on the retreatants. The retreatants must develop the material according to their own insights.

Third, only two contemplations that contain new material are presented each day; the other three periods of prayer are repetitions. Ignatius indicates that we are to think about the points as we fall asleep, and that we are to do the first contemplation in the middle of the night and the second in the morning. Thus we spend one half the night sleeping on the material for each contemplation [204 and 208]. So he arranges these in such a way as to give our unconscious mind plenty of time to mull over, develop and select what is most appropriate for us.

Finally, Ignatius says that we should pray over a very few things. He has indicated that once we find what we are looking for on any point we should stay quietly with that and not move on [76]. Perhaps the admonition of Ignatius in the Fourth Week is applicable here also:

> Though in all the contemplations a definite number of points is given . . . the one who is contemplating may make use of more or fewer as seems better for him. For this reason it will be very useful before entering on the contemplation to foresee and determine a definite number of points that are to be used [228].

We have a small example in the first contemplation of this week. It is introduced as "Christ our Lord goes from Bethany to Jerusalem and the Last Supper" [190], but when Ignatius develops the points he focuses only on three incidents within the Last Supper [289].

Not only do the various contemplations of Ignatius contain a number of incidents, but each incident contains a lot of points that could be meditated on and that could be variously interpreted. Meditating on the Agony in the Garden, for example, we might have our attention drawn to the mental anguish of Christ, the fear of physical suffering yet to come, feelings of betrayal by a friend, pain because the apostles do not support him, God's apparently adverse will, sorrow caused by our sinfulness, a sense of failure, or maybe even just the difficulty of staying awake and praying in the middle of the night. What will we pick? We will unconsciously pick what we need to pray about, what we need to let go of; we will select a form of suffering that arises out of our own past experience, our present attachments, and our future fears.

This is how we might pick out things to meditate upon in general. We read Scripture and one verse stands out, as if written in bold-face type, and it "grabs" us. That is what we should be meditating on. It grabs us because our own psyches under grace know what they need.

Union with Christ Through Love and Compassion

Now all this may seem very negative. Let us take a look at a few positive elements. The dynamic of the week is driven by the grace of God, by the strength of our commitment to the election, and most of all by our love of and commitment to Christ, and by the very strong affective bond with Christ which has been growing over the course of the first two weeks. That deep love is an essential of the Third Week. It is the very driving force of the Third Week without which not much will happen, for it keeps us bound to Christ as he progresses towards his death. As in the third degree of humility, we are not choosing suffering, but to be with Christ in his suffering. If we love anything more than Christ, we will not leave it behind when the Third Week brings us to the point where we must surrender it. We are presupposing here a love of Christ stronger than all other loves, or a love that is capable of becoming that strong during the course of the week.

Our love during this week is such that we will tend to think more of the Lord than of ourselves. We may meditate upon the passion as part of a first, second, or third-week dynamic. In the First Week our attention is consciously on our selves and our sins; in the Second Week we look at Christ's life and ministry as a model for our own, containing lessons we should learn; in the Third Week the reference to self, to our sins, to our suffering, even to our election, our attachments, and our fears is swallowed up in our attention to Christ who goes to his death, whom we love and with whom we desire to stay.

We have also been talking perhaps a bit too much about our subjectivity, without noticing that the very nature of compassion demands objectivity. Even though what we focus on may be guided by our own dispositions, true compassion demands that our attention be primarily on someone else who suffers. Even though suffering can have a personal reference to ourselves in ways we may not want to ascribe to Christ, nevertheless, in general, the suffering will be seen and understood as a suffering of the Lord, grounded in the Gospel and in his life. And this is right because Christ has been tried in all suffering and temptations like us (Heb 4:15, 2:17-18). On another level the sufferings of the retreatant are in fact the sufferings of the Body of Christ of which the retreatant is a member; they make up and complete what may be lacking to the suffering of the Body (Col 1:24). So we enter into a suffering that is not just ours and not just Christ's, but a suffering that is mysteriously ours and Christ's at the same time.

In each of the contemplations of the Third Week, we are united more closely with Christ through compassionate suffering. But this compassion is more than sentiment; it reaches deeply into the volitional level of our existence; it constitutes an implicit choice and continued commitment. All through this week we are led to a crossroads; every contemplation is a crossroads. We are constantly faced with a choice. In the first two weeks of the retreat we stood at a crossroads and saw two ways: one was the way of sin that led to death and destruction; the other is the way of Christ that leads to life. But as we start the Third Week, there has been a dramatic reversal: Christ walks now the road to death, not the path that leads to the goods of this life. He abandons the path that leads to temporal happiness, comfort, popularity, and success. In each contemplation of the Third Week, we must choose among our various loves. To stay with the Lord we must let go of other things; we must surrender and abandon them affectively.

This choice determines who we are and who we will be. It decides what will and will not be part of our existence, what we will live to and die to. Paul describes the passion of Christ not so much in physical as in psychological terms when he says: "His death was death to sin, once for all; his life is life for God. In the same way, you must consider yourselves dead to sin but alive for God in Christ Jesus" (Rom 6:10-11). This is the kind of death that the Third Week invites us to and the kind of life that we discover in the Fourth Week.

Now, just as the shadow side of a person is represented in a dream by some symbol, in these contemplations the implicit choice is frequently symbolized by the presence of some foil that represents an alternative to the following of Christ. One might contrast the sleeping apostles with the vigilant Christ, Peter's denial with Christ's affirmation of his messiahship, Christ's failure and the success of the enemy, Christ's meekness and the brutality of his persecutors, Christ's death and those who survive. In the dynamic of the Third Week, it is important for us to identify with Christ; to identify with those who abandon Christ or who cause his suffering may be a sign that our attention has returned to ourselves and our sin, and that we are engaged in first-week repentance. Deep compassion, however, involves identification with Christ, a choice of him over all other loves, and an affective renunciation of the particular good involved in the meditation.

The Order of Topics of Contemplation

In each of the contemplations of the Third Week, compassionate suffering with Christ is implicitly a choice of Christ and a death to some aspect of our old selves. Let us take a look now at what is involved in the dynamic movement from one contemplation to another and at some of the principles that determine more concretely why we select certain forms of suffering to pray about.

There is a certain order rooted in the objective history of the passion. The agony in the garden comes first, the death and burial at the end. At the beginning there is fear, looking forward to the future; at the end there is final dissolution, looking forward to no future at all. The suffering of Christ is seen early in the week as physical discomfort, cold, weariness; but in the face of death such minor sufferings cannot be the topic of prayer. The subject matter may make betrayal by a friend, the opposition of religious and political authority, or abandonment by God a fairly obvious choice for contemplation.

But our subjective dispositions will also help determine the order of sufferings that we consider. The retreatant in this week is very much like an onion; every contemplation peels off a layer until there is nothing left. The retreatant comes to the contemplation already constituted in a certain way. The first layer that is going to be taken off is the layer that is at the top. There is something in the psychic build-up of each of us that determines the order in which we will approach the possible sufferings that we could consider.

Yet, because our human natures are so much alike, even though the order will vary from one person to another, there ought to be the same general order. I believe that generally what is most external, most conscious, easiest to cope with and what may be considered the weakest attachment is dealt with first. And these are not four totally different things, but there is a certain consistency among them so that we will focus on one form of suffering that responds to these four criteria. By a gradual progression the retreatant moves closer to the center of his being, to what is most personal, most repressed, most difficult and the strongest attachment. The last barrier to fall will be letting go of concern for our own existence, facing the fear of death, and surrendering all things.

As we approach topics for contemplation, we are too sincere and generous to select what is trivial, what is not really suffering for us at this particular point. We will not waste time looking at a good we do not desire or a loss we are already reconciled to. But we still have an instinct for survival and an inclination to avoid painful change. In the tension between this movement to salvage as much as we can of ourselves and the sincere desire to suffer with Christ, we will pick a form of suffering that is significant, but may not yet strike to the very core of our existence.

We also are aware, unconsciously at least, of our strengths and weaknesses, and of our ability to cope with various attachments. We will not choose too much below our ability, since that would be insincere; nor too much beyond our ability since that would invite, even intend, failure and would be insincere in its own way. We will choose rather something that is challenging but possible.

So amid these various pressures of our own sense of suffering and what the text says about Christ, our desire and our fear of entering into the suffering of Christ, our balance of self-surrender and self-preservation, our selection of what is challenging but not impossible, we shall pick and concentrate on a point of the passion. And this point will be a suffering for Christ and for us, an element that could endanger our election and which we must become willing to lose, a place where we are called upon to die and where we can die with the grace of God.

If we fail to become reconciled, to die to whatever good Christ is being deprived of then the area remains an unresolved problem. In fact it becomes worse. Because we are aware of our refusal and because we are sincere in our choice of Christ, we should be bothered by this failure. In the next contemplation our thoughts will come back to the same point. We recall that Ignatius tells us to concentrate on what gave us consolation or desolation [118 and 204], and we can be fairly sure of sadness over this kind of failure. He says as well that if we feel repugnance to something, we should pray all the more insistently for it [157].

We are, however, motivated by deep and sincere love, and it is within our ability to cope with the suffering we have selected. So it is likely that eventually with grace we shall succeed in reconciling ourselves to whatever loss we fear. We may experience some consolation because of this and may return to the point to let that detachment deepen and strengthen, but the area is no longer problematic, and the Lord is moving on to his death. We cannot remain behind. Our emphases shift and we move on to another and a deeper level of our beings.

Progression Between Various Levels

There may be a general pattern to these levels: a movement from an external, physical dimension to a social and then to a personal or spiritual dimension. This general scheme follows the scheme indicated by Ignatius in the Two Standards—poverty, insults, deep humility—[146], and elsewhere in the *Exercises* [9, 23, 98, 116, 142, 147, 166–167]. It likewise follows in general the history of the passion and what in most personalities may constitute the passage from what is on the surface to what is deepest. But each of these can be broken down even more. The external might include poverty, physical discomfort, and various kinds of pain; the social could include betrayal, desertion, loss of friendship, hatred, lack of esteem, rejection by religious or civil authority, rejection by people in general, scorn, contempt; the personal might comprise self-doubt, failure, fear and anxiety, impending doom, abandonment by God, final annihilation and hopelessness. Each retreatant is going to flesh out the general scheme in a unique fashion.

The different levels or topics may be interrelated in such a way that the deeper ones will serve as supports when the lesser ones are renounced. When we have let go of one good on which we relied, we tend to rely more on what we have left. We might, for example, rely on friends when we have lost our possessions, on our self-esteem when we have lost friends, on God when we have lost hope even in ourselves. At the same time our need for security is greater, our fear of losing what we have left increases, and we become concerned about our new supports. This greater reliance and greater concern focus our attention on this deeper good or suffering and almost guarantee it will become the topic of the following contemplation. Thus the contemplation moves deeper and deeper, ever closer to the center of our being and concern.

As we progress we come to each new form of suffering more experienced in renunciation, more able to cope with this suffering than we were before, more convinced of the contingency of created goods, and more bound in love to Christ. By little and little we are led on to die to ourselves and our world until we have completely entered into the death of the Lord.

Death and Resurrection with Christ

The perfection of that dying should be reached in the contemplations on the death and burial that take place on the sixth day of the Third Week.

The contemplation on the death of Christ involves the total renunciation of all things and all attachments, whether we have considered them explicitly or not; it involves a death to the good as well as the evil. We have no insurance policies that rob death of its fearfulness and make of this final dissolution a mere momentary passage from one life to a better one. If we have entered into Christ's abandonment by God and into the fifth point of each contemplation, how the divinity hides itself [196], then we will face death with faith, but also with the doubts and risks that faith involves.

The contemplation on the burial is one of the most important contemplations of this week. It brings us out of suffering and pain into a stillness where there is no longer any desire or fear, no rejoicing over good, no sorrow over pain. The burial reinforces this death to the world and indifference to all its pleasures and pains. Our life is now Christ alone, the dead and buried Christ. We may say with Claudel

> I have descended with You into the tomb. . . .
> There have I lain without motion,
> and the confines of Your tomb
> Have become the confines of the Universe.

It is to this utter stillness and motionlessness of death that the inexorable progression of the Third Week has brought us. These contemplations are made on the sixth day, and the rest of the day is silence. Even though on every other day Ignatius has said there will be two repetitions and an application of the senses on the same material, he now stops repeating this instruction and gives no indication of anything else happening on the sixth day [208]. It is as if any contemplation here would disrupt the silence of the tomb into which we have entered.

This silence is itself the goal to which the week has been leading. It is death to the world, death to self-will, and freedom from everything that can undo the election. It is the perfection of Ignatian indifference and the term toward which the meditations on the Three Classes and the Three Kinds of Humility have been leading. And it is out of this silence that there will come an experience of the risen Christ.

The seventh day begins with a review of the whole passion [208], and Ignatius provides for even three more days to be spent on the entire passion [209]. These provisions are to complete the dynamic of the week if that proves necessary; they provide, I believe, for the completion of any renunciation that may not yet have taken place.

The rest of the seventh day is devoted to contemplation on the dead and buried Christ and on the desolation, sorrow, and fatigue of Mary and the disciples. Properly understood, these contemplations also bring us to the silence of the tomb. The purpose is not to review the history of how the body came to be buried or to look at what is happening to the soul of Christ in Sheol. The first is an invitation to enter into the darkness and silence of the tomb and to watch the soulless body of the Lord, not to see anything happening, but precisely to see nothing happening. The other reflection of the day, looking at the weariness and fatigue of Mary and the apostles, is also a contemplation on burial. They go about their activities in a stupefied daze, for their hearts are buried with Christ. They have entered into the deep silence that is the sign of deep grief. These last days of the week then are days of stillness in which, despite any activity, the retreatant lies dead beside the dead Lord.

This is the silence of Holy Saturday that must interpose between deep grief and great joy. Out of this stillness we shall experience resurrection and Christ who is now alive. We may discover the risen Christ, peacefully or exuberantly, in the stillness of the last days of week three. And, like Zen satori, it very well may come outside of prayer; we may awaken to the power of the risen Lord, not while concentrating on his past historical apparitions, but while we attend to the reality of our own daily lives where the risen Lord is present. The contemplations of the Fourth Week are a further stimulus for us to open our eyes and to see who surrounds us and fills us with life, who saves us despite our worst fears, and despite all suffering, pain, and loss.

But the Fourth Week dynamic does not arise because the director decided we should pray about resurrection. It does not come about because we have decided to pray about something else. It comes about because we have entered into the death of the Lord, and once we have done that, the outcome is inevitable. The Fourth Week is not an experience that there is life as well as death, but that precisely out of the death to sin arises life to God and that by being buried with Christ we shall also rise with him.

This interpretation of the Third Week should not be understood as talking about things that are unique to the *Exercises*. The theology of monasticism or of the religious life is a theology of dying with Christ in order to enter into his life. And the theology of baptism is a theology of the burial of Christians with the Lord in order to share his resurrection. This is the same mystery that is working in the Christian life that is really being lived, in ascetical and mystical theology. It is the mystery we celebrate in the Eucharist, the death and resurrection of the Lord and our participation in it. It is a dynamic that is alive in us every day in all of our choices, in all of our distractions in prayer, and in all of our temptations.

Only by entering totally into the death of Christ can we also enter into his risen joy. Good Friday and Easter are really one event; it will just take time, once buried with Christ, for us to realize what we have entered into. And having found Christ we shall find again as well the whole cosmos of which he is the center, the source and the final end.[2]

NOTES

[1]On this see Brian O'Leary, S.J., "Third and Fourth Week: What the Directories Say," *The Way: Supplement*, spring 1987, 3–20, especially 11. Also: *Directorium Exercitiorum Spiritualium (1544–1599)*, MHSI, vol 76, 729.

[2]The substance of this paper was first published by the author in *The Way*, supplement 34, autumn 1978; it is gratefully used here with the permission of the editors of *The Way*.

8

The *Spiritual Exercises*, Their Adaptation in Daily Life, and the Laity

Shannon Rupp Barnes

An introduction to the Spiritual Exercises *today that does not take into account their relation to laity in today's Church is at best inadequate. More-over, as indicated elsewhere, the* Exercises *are not the patrimony of reli-gious orders in general and of the Jesuits in particular. They distill the experience of Ignatius as a layman. As a layman he directed many lay people through the experience of the* Exercises *long before he was ordained a priest, much less became involved in the founding of the Society of Jesus. Shannon Barnes' contribution offers a fine, brief summary of the opportunity, suita-bility and requirements for lay people making the* Spiritual Exercises. *More-over, she explains their adaptation in an open setting of daily work life as distinguished from the experience of thirty days in a setting of silence and solitude. This is simply what Ignatius himself envisaged as a needed adap-tation for lay people in his introductory observations or annotations [19] to the* Exercises.

As we look at the world today and especially at our American culture, we realize that we are in a time of many transitions and quick changes. We see a fast moving world with many demands, pressures, and stresses, but also one which offers much in return. All of us are very much immersed in and affected by this world. We are also increasingly aware, that we are a part of a Church tradition that has changed radically in the past twenty-five years, especially when we consider the four unchanging centuries be-tween Trent and Vatican II.

Since the laity make up 98 percent of the Catholic Church, one very significant area of change in the Church is the role of the laity. Today many articles and numerous books discuss the mission of the lay person, God's universal call to holiness, the nature of "lay spirituality," and the role of the lay person in today's Church. Since Vatican II, we see lay people taking on new roles and responsibilities. These represent new challenges for each of us, both personal and communal.

One challenge that more and more lay people are hearing and responding to is that of spiritual growth. In searching to answer this call, they are discovering that many of the spiritual traditions or schools of spirituality have a monastic character. That is, they say that for spiritual growth leading to union with God, one must find solitude and in some way be removed from the world—an impossibility for those who live in a secular world, and wear many hats: professional, provider, parent, family, manager, volunteer, friend, parishioner, to name a few. The questions of laity interested in spiritual growth are thus "where and how do we best direct our energy? How can we grow spiritually and function in our multifaceted roles?"

In the history of spirituality, Ignatius of Loyola, while still a layman, introduced a new, unique, "apostolic" spirituality, expressed through the *Spiritual Exercises* as "contemplation in action." Ignatius emphasized praise, reverence, service, and a "finding God in all things." Rather than withdrawing from the world, the seeker of God goes out into the world to meet him in Jesus Christ in the ordinary, everyday people and events that are the "stuff" of their ordinary, everyday lives. Such a spirituality stresses the importance of a discerning heart, which recognizes God in each person and in the community.

Before his ordination at age forty-six, Ignatius, very much man of the world, reflected upon his own spiritual journey, especially his experience of conversion, and from that experience he developed most of what came to be the *Exercises.* Reading his *Autobiography,* one can trace in it his awareness of his interiority, the periods of his consolation and desolation, and his development of the rules for discernment of spirits. Today discernment has significance especially for lay people or for any persons who, in the "busy-ness" of life, wish to grow in their relationship with God.

As people search for God and for meaning in our complex world, the *Exercises* and Ignatian spirituality offer much to deepen one's relationships with God, with one's immediate human community, and with the concerns of the world. My reaction to Ignatian spirituality is that it fits my own personal experience and reality. It is ordinary, it is day-to-day, and yet it is dynamic. The experience of the *Exercises* is that of a process, not simply of static mental exercises.

The complete *Spiritual Exercises* are most often experienced in a thirty-day enclosed retreat, removed from the pressures and distractions of life. Ignatius realized, however, that not everyone could take that much time away from family and responsibilities. He wrote into the *Exercises* a special annotation which provides for the *Exercises* in Daily Life, or the 19th Annotation Retreat, as it is sometimes called.

> I may want to help a retreatant of talent and proper disposition through the full Exercises, but carried on in the face of normal occupations and living conditions for the extent of the whole retreat. As director I should determine, along with the retreatant, the amount of time possible each day for prayer and divide up the matter accordingly. If an hour and a half can be secured daily by the retreatant, the retreat could progress slowly, with almost a single point providing enough material for such a length of prayer. For example, in the First Exercise of the First Week, each single example of sin might provide the matter to be considered in prayer for that day. So, too, in the mysteries of Our Lord's life, I may find it helpful to have the retreatant return to the same mystery for three or four days in succession (F 17, cf. [19]).

For most laity, as well as for many diocesan priests and religious who desire the experience of the *Exercises*, but do not have the luxury of time for an enclosed thirty-day retreat the 19th Annotation retreat is a fruitful, authentic alternative.

For the director of the *Exercises* in either mode, Annotation 18 is a significant directive:

> It is my role as a director to adapt the Spiritual Exercises to each retreatant, in view of his or her age and maturity, education and also potential and talents. I should decide what exercises would prove useless or even harmful to a retreatant because of a lack of physical strength or natural ability as well as what exercises would benefit and perhaps challenge a retreatant who is properly disposed and endowed. I may often discover that a retreatant at this particular time of life has neither the ability nor sometimes the desire to go beyond what is ordinarily described as the exercises of the First Week. So, too, I should make the judgment whether the full *Exercises* would be profitable to a particular retreatant at this time. Because the Exercises are a limited instrument through which God can work, I should be aware that many persons would not be able to enter well into the Exercises. . . . (F 15, cf. [18]).

The point is that each person will go through this experience uniquely. The role of the director then, is to adapt the *Exercises* to the needs of the individual.

Let us look at some of the practical considerations of making the 19th Annotation retreat or the *Exercises* in Daily Life.

What Is The Time Involved in Making This Retreat?

An individual desiring to make this retreat should decide with the director how much time he or she can commit to prayer each day, given the other jobs and responsibilities in everyday life. Most often the time allotted to prayer would be between one to one and a half hours. This time may need to be divided into half-hour or forty-five minute periods.

If a person is properly disposed or ready to make the *Exercises,* one can expect that the retreat would extend over a period of thirty weeks. It could take seven months, twelve months, or even longer depending on the situation. Some directors may choose to contract a certain time, e.g., thirty weeks, just as one would contract in an enclosed retreat. Others may leave the time span open-ended, so that the dynamics determine the time span of the *Exercises.* Often directors will advocate beginning the *Exercises* in Daily Life in the fall in order that the retreat follows the liturgical seasons. This, however, is not an absolute.

Another time commitment would be to the once-a-week meeting with the director to review what is happening in prayer. After the director and retreatant discern and evaluate together, the director determines whether the retreatant is ready to go on to the next exercise.

Readiness for Making the Exercises

A director trying to assess a person's readiness for the *Exercises* needs to have some knowledge of the individual's experience of spiritual direction over a span of at least six months to a year. "Readiness" for making the *Exercises* is not measured by someone else's enthusiasm. In my involvement with spiritual direction, in directing the *Exercises,* and in training others in this ministry, I have frequently heard people who were very excited about their own experience relate that this is something everyone should do, a sort of "Let's go for it" attitude. In their eagerness they would attempt to lead others into the *Exercises* immediately, only to find them not ready.

Similarly, sometimes a person has heard that making the *Exercises* is a "good thing to do," and all of a sudden he or she wants to "jump on the bandwagon." This doing the "in" thing is not necessarily "bad," for one can still reap benefits from the experience. However, preparation, motivation, and desire are key components of the experience of the *Exercises.*

Another lack of readiness is simply the lack of a regular, disciplined prayer life, or the presence of a lot of "baggage" or obstacles that get in the way of openness to God's work. Healing may be needed. A person may be going through a high stress time in life and cannot enter into the experience of the *Exercises* in a healthy or wholehearted way.

A person who desires to make the *Exercises* needs the ability to deal with personal and relational issues or blocks. Someone who has recently gone through a "death" experience, such as the "death" of a marriage or the actual physical loss of a loved one, may not be ready to enter the intense experience that the dynamics of the *Exercises* becomes. Most probably the individual needs first to work through the grieving process.

The most important readiness is the prospective retreatant's sense of being loved and lovable, a sense that making the *Exercises* ordinarily deepens. That is not always easy. In a culture where self-images are frequently distorted, where many people do not see themselves as loved and lovable, on-going spiritual direction may be necessary to assist an individual in this area preparatory to making the *Exercises*.

One example of the importance of readiness came from a man who shared with me that he now wished his spiritual director had not led him into making the *Exercises* so early in his experience of spiritual direction. Although he had some good experiences with the *Exercises*, he realized in hindsight that as a recovering alcoholic with many "scripts" to work through, both personally and in his relationship with God, making the *Exercises* when he did was premature. Now after two years of on-going spiritual direction and healing, he felt much more ready and free to enter fully into their dynamic.

Another individual who was "ready" began the *Exercises* in Daily Life. At that time he was employed full time as an engineer, had family responsibilities, was attending graduate school, was a participant in our internship training program for spiritual/retreat directors, and on weekends helped minister at a local parish. As a "committed" Christian and retreatant, he found himself getting up at 3:30 a.m. to get in his prayer times. After a few weeks on this schedule, he stopped in my office and commented that he was not sure he could continue the *Exercises* with the many demands on his time and energy. I suggested he discuss this with his spiritual director and strongly recommended that he wait until the multiple demands in his life had lessened before committing himself to the *Exercises*. Spiritually he was ready, but the timing was not right; he was jeopardizing his health and draining his energy.

The spiritual director faced with individuals desiring to make the *Exercises* must ask these important questions: is the person ready? is the time right? what are the present pressures, obstacles, or hindrances? is the person sufficiently free and open to love?

Who Can Direct the Spiritual Exercises?

The selection of a director is an important consideration for one wishing to make the *Exercises* in Daily Life. A spiritual director who has not made the complete *Exercises* should not direct them. This seems to be an unwritten rule that most qualified directors follow. There are movements unique in the process of the *Exercises,* especially in the sensitive area of discernment of spirits, so that unless the director has had personal experience of the *Exercises,* he or she may not have an understanding of the dynamics operating in the retreatant.

Besides having made the *Exercises* personally, some other qualifications for a director of the *Exercises* would include a sound experiential knowledge of spiritual direction and the dynamics of the *Exercises,* expertise in discernment acquired by a habit of personal discernment, and the experience of helping others discern.

Most directors of the *Exercises* in Daily Life limit the number of retreatants they will guide in a year's time. They realize that their commitment as a director can be a demanding experience, both in the intensity of the retreat and in the time necessary to meet the retreatant each week over an extended period of months.

Impact of the Retreat

Many people making the *Exercises* find it a time of "special grace." In almost every experience, they have a sense—a realization—of the integration of prayer and life. They do see God in all things. They encounter God in the faces of their children, in the cup of coffee with a neighbor, in the "pat on the back" from a colleague, in the warm smile of the cashier. For them "The world is charged with the glory of God," as Gerard Manley Hopkins put it.

Another impact of the retreat is a deepened sense of God's love for each person and for all creation. As people experience God's love, they become more aware of the need more fully to participate as co-workers in the care of God's people and God's world.

Most people who have made the *Exercises* see more deeply with the "eyes" of faith, develop a fuller appreciation of on-going discernment, and acquire the gift of a discerning heart. In everyday, ordinary life their questions are "What is the most loving thing to do? How does Jesus want me to be in this situation?" By using the Consciousness Examen within or outside the *Exercises,* the individual becomes more reflective. Reflection on experience plays a very important part in a person's growth in relationship with God.

The *Spiritual Exercises* can also bring the retreatant to a more intimate relationship with Jesus, the Risen Lord. Having entered deeply into the mysteries of Jesus' life, the retreatant experiences these mysteries as living and meaningful for today. Retreatants develop a real sense of the way in which God calls each person uniquely, and how that call has a communal effect. Each one is called as an individual and as a member of community.

The contribution Ignatius of Loyola has made in the *Spiritual Exercises* reflects his own experience, but that experience resonates within each person open to receive God's grace and enter into this dynamic experience.

9

The Risen Lord and the Contemplation on Love

John A. McGrail, S.J.

In discussions of the Spiritual Exercises, *the Fourth Week especially, but even the Contemplation of Love concluding the* Exercises, *do not often get the consideration that they deserve. This presentation was somewhat different in style than the earlier ones in the series. Whereas most of the other lectures operated on a plane of discourse that related to contemporary spiritual theology or historical research on the* Exercises, *John McGrail's seemed more a distillation of his many years of experience in directing people in the* Exercises *and in spiritual growth generally. It appeared to some at times to be more akin to a sermon that was very well received. As such it makes an excellent conclusion to the chapters here on different facets of the* Exercises *besides presenting some helpful insights on encountering the risen Lord.*

The Fourth Week of the Exercises

I am not sure about the content of the talks that have preceded this one, but I am reasonably sure that practically everyone has spoken about the purpose of the *Spiritual Exercises* of St. Ignatius. Put simply, the *Exercises* aim at freedom. This is something that today should be especially significant. When we follow them right to the end, they should give us the tools to keep regaining the freedom from all those disorders or disinclinations that entangle us and trip us up. They should give us freedom to reach out and embrace God, find out what he wants me to do, what he wants me to become, and to work along with him in becoming the best kind of person that I can possibly be.

I am talking here not so much about the resurrection as about the Fourth Week of the *Exercises*. If we make them properly, we should end up seeing that Jesus Christ is the dominant figure in our history. It is not Gorbachev, nor is it President Reagan, but Jesus Christ who is the pre-eminent person in our ongoing history. In addition, I would find in making the *Exercises* what precisely God's plan is for my own insertion into this continuing history of which Christ is the master and Lord.

That obviously makes us look ahead and not look back. Robert Kennedy said that not many men or women can completely revolutionize the course of events in their lives. As we look back over history there are a few that have done this: people like Washington, Lincoln, or Martin Luther King. But, Kennedy continued, everybody ought to aim at bending the course of events for the better. That is something that everyone can do. The *Exercises* should help me to find out what might be my particular insertion into this stream of history.

However, everybody who has made them knows that there is always a problem of following up on the *Spiritual Exercises*. Time and again, people say, "Oh, everything went very well in my retreat and I was very stirred by the *Exercises*; I had my eyes set on a goal and I was going to accomplish it, but then something happened. I wish I could bring back those glorious days when I was in the midst of my retreat." There is a lot of psychology involved in the keeping of resolutions. Sometimes the problem is that people do not have a director to whom they can open themselves. There are other problems in prayer, of course, and a thousand things that can make us unstable. I think one of the main problems is that people simply do not make the Fourth Week of the *Exercises*. This is very often the weak link in a person's retreat—the proper making of the Fourth Week. Yet it is a problem not often adverted to.

Now there are a lot of reasons for this. In the past, in our own history and in our theology, we tended to look backwards. We looked back on the crucifixion influenced by the theology of St. Anselm that placed much stress upon the satisfactory aspects of the death of Christ, i.e., how to atone for our sins. In separating the crucifixion from the rest of Christ's life, however, and looking back all the time, we tended to give away one of the great advantages of Christianity. The Christian faith does not live in the past at all. Christianity always lives in the present and in the future. We let people like the Communists steal away from us this whole idea of evolving a better world and being part of it and bending the course of history.

Some of that comes from our looking back all the time at the resurrection. Some of it comes from the fact that there is not very much writing about the Fourth Week. Sometimes, moreover, people just came to that point in their retreat tired. They simply went at the Fourth Week in the same way they did the Third. In about 1960 F. X. Durrwell's book on the resurrection appeared in this country.[1] It began to develop a whole new attitude among priests and religious concerning the resurrection. About a year later David Stanley brought out his doctoral dissertation on St. Paul and the resurrection and the future life.[2] All this has given us a deeper insight into religion and specifically into the theology of the *Exercises*.

Let me illustrate by two devotional practices. Up until a few years ago devotion to the Sacred Heart flourished. Catholics looked upon Christ as imprisoned, helpless, deserving reparation, which we tended to translate into mere sympathy. However, the latest letter of the present pope on the subject tells us that real reparation to the Sacred Heart means that we see this Kingdom in ruins around us and the Lord calls us to help rebuild his Kingdom. It is a present and a future work. What can I do? How can I help bring this about?

Another example is the way Christians think of the main event of Christianity as Christmas, as if that is our main feast. It marks the day Christ was born; we keep looking back on it and we touch upon it as a historical event. Thus Easter gets passed over. The great event of Christianity, however, is Christ's resurrection, Jesus' being alive, and his continuing to build up his kingdom. It is, after all, through the resurrection that Christ is asking everybody that ever hears him at all to participate with him in building up his Kingdom, which is going to spread throughout the world. We see how little we have pursued this kind of thinking in the Church.

The basic thrust of the Fourth Week of the *Exercises* is that we are going to be redeemed even now in every aspect of our life. That is what our contemplations should tell us. Above all we must enter into the Fourth Week as an ongoing event. If we simply enter into it as if we are looking back on past historical events, as we may have done in other contemplations, then I think the Fourth Week of the *Exercises* becomes weak and, to some extent, ineffective.

As most of you know who have made the *Exercises*, the instructions Ignatius gives at the beginning of the Fourth Week are decidedly brief and this presents us with a problem. He seems to take it for granted that intuitively we know what we are doing by this time and that our contemplations are such that we can truly enter into the risen life of Christ in the way that he envisages. As usual, Ignatius starts in the first prelude by giving a history of whatever we are going to contemplate [219]. Here he says, peculiarly enough, that what we are going to do is contemplate how Christ dies, was buried, soul and body separated, how he descended into hell. (We are using "hell" not in the sense in which we often speak of it. "He descended into the nether world, into the realm of the dead," would be a more exact expression.) Christ released those who had gone before him, returned, rose from the dead, then he appeared first to his mother. He says that is the history that he wants us to think about.

Oddly enough, in another part of the *Exercises*, Ignatius says that in presenting a meditation or contemplation, the director should be very terse in suggesting material for prayer, sticking only to "the solid foundation of facts" [2]. Ignatius seems to say, "Do not be wandering off into a lot of imaginary things that are not in the Scriptures." At this point we might want to ask Ignatius, "Why are you saying this? It does not say anything in the Gospel about Christ appearing to his mother. Why do you want us to contemplate that?" And Ignatius says to us, "Of course, it does not say anything about it in Scripture. But it also says in Scripture, 'Are you also without understanding?' "[3] He simply takes this for granted and it is the only time in the *Exercises* he becomes a bit apologetic or acidic in handling criticism.

Then he gives us in the second prelude a "composition of the place" so that we are situated in a concrete setting [220]. He would have us notice the details of the sepulcher, look at our Lady's room, where she is going to be, and how we would pray in that situation. Then in the third prelude he tells us, as he always does at the beginning of prayer, to ask for something that we want [221]. Here he would have us ask for a great sense of joy and triumph in Christ's glorious resurrection. We are truly not asking something for ourselves. It is a tremendously generous thing to ask to share in Christ's joy. We know it is not hard to share in somebody else's sorrow. We go to a funeral home, for example, at the death of someone. We get that sympathetic feeling about a friend's loss. We can easily cry. Still it is very hard to enter into feeling the joy of someone. We can say, "Oh, I am very glad for you. I congratulate you. I am proud of you." Yet really to feel and enter into the joy of someone is not easy. Still that is what Ignatius tells us ought to be the kind of prayer that we make here.

Ignatius then reminds us again to contemplate the persons, words, and actions [222. Cf. 194] as he did in the second and third weeks. In other words, we become part of the whole mystery. He then adds two points. First, in the resurrection we should think about how the divinity of Christ manifests itself. The contemplation of Jesus appearing to the Blessed Virgin at the outset of the Fourth Week is given, I think, because Ignatius wants us to concentrate upon what the resurrection meant to Christ himself. The second point Ignatius suggests is that we should always think of the risen Christ as a consoler too. He consoles the people that we would console in our life. When somebody consoles someone, if they are really sincere, if that person has a serious illness, cancer for example, they do not tell him that he does not have it. They support him. They share with him and they tell him they will help him through this difficult problem. And when Christ consoles us he does the same thing, too. He shares with us. He does not tell us he is going to take away the pain or the suffering. He is going to support us and he is going to help us through it.

I think that such is really an evidence of sincere religion. Sometimes people will falsely speak of religion and tell us, "Just pray, you will get rid of the problem." But I think that when we are honest we tell people, "Just pray, and God will help you with your problem." This is a totally different thing. Many times he does not take the problem away. He may show us various ways in which we can handle it, how we can go about it and overcome it, and how through the midst of it we can achieve peace and a great deal of satisfaction, but God does not take those things away, as God did not take them away from his Son either.

So, when he comes to his mother as a consoler, and when we think about him and his resurrection, what did that mean to him? To be alive! He had been dead. He had said that he had a baptism with which he was going to be baptized; he was on edge until he accomplished it (Luke 12:49-50). Now suddenly it is over. He can look back and say it is done. Now he has to make this clear to these people around him, what his being here really means. That is when the emphasis should be on our prayer in the Fourth Week—Jesus Christ is alive. He is here. He is present.

There is a peculiar character to the risen Christ's appearances. Before his death, the apostles did not have faith. They could *see* Jesus of Nazareth. In fact, they had a problem almost opposite to the one we have. A theologian in our times has said that he thinks that most Christians believe that Jesus Christ is truly God. But very few of them believe that he was and is truly human. I think that he is right.

We find it very hard to attribute to Jesus of Nazareth fear, doubt, hesitation, worry, and anxiety, to look at him as he really is in the Scripture and as Mark especially shows him to be. As the apostles looked at him, however, they could see quite clearly that he was very much a human being. They watched him eat, bathe in the lake, fall asleep, get irritated, and do many other very human everyday things. They had a problem in trying to see he was divine. They could say, as some of them did: you are the Messiah. But what did that mean to them really, when they spoke of him? How could they possibly grasp what it meant to be the Son of God, to be the Lord of all creation, to be the master of time, the master of history? How could they possibly see that? So, when he rose from the dead, he had to build up in them a faith in whom he was.

Little by little he began to teach them what his presence really means. He appears, as we know, first to the women. He tells them to go and speak to the apostles. Then he himself comes to this group from which he is about to build his Church, and he tries to tell them something about who he really is. Why was it not enough for him, having risen from the dead, simply to appear once and let it go at that? Just as, in a crude analogy for example, a magician might saw somebody in half and then afterwards show us the whole person. Once—that is enough. What is he trying to tell them about his presence? What is he trying to tell us about his presence? We have to keep thinking about it over and over again, because I think it makes all the difference in the world how we handle our Christianity, what we do about it, how this paschal faith begins to grow in us.

First, we cannot read the Gospel stories of the resurrection without getting a sense that those encounters are somewhat unreal (cf. Luke 24:16, 37). When Jesus appears in the midst of the apostles, one of them will say: "I think it is Jesus, but there is something unfamiliar about him." There is an ethereal quality about him. Jesus presses the point. He says to Thomas: "Look, I am not a ghost. Come and put your finger into My wounds, your hand into my side. I am not a spirit that is just conjured up. I am real. This is me. I am present before you body and soul. I am this human being here" (cf. John 20:24-29). Yet he is different. There was something about him that was unrecognizable. They needed that reassurance all the time, and he would give it to them.

He came back again a week later when Thomas was there. Thomas had said, "That is impossible. Nobody comes back from the dead." Later on when Paul would try to talk to the Greeks about it, the Athenians said the same thing (AA 17:22ff). It is not possible. And that is our problem today. A lot of people just start with the impossibility. No one can come back from the dead. Therefore Jesus did not come back from the dead.

The sudden appearances of Jesus are strange events indeed. He comes suddenly. He disappears quickly. The Gospel never explains how or why it happens. I think the reason is because the evangelists did not know how or why it happened. Suddenly the disciples knew that Christ was present in their midst. In the scene at Emmaus (Luke 24:13-35), Jesus had been conversing for some time with the two disciples—probably husband and wife. They did not recognize him. At supper as he breaks the bread they see clearly who he is. At once he vanished from their sight—as though he faded away.

There is no explanation for this at all. But the Gospels describe how people felt. Mary Magdalene is standing in front of the sepulcher (John 20:11-18), looking at it and thinking that the body was stolen, perhaps by grave robbers, perhaps by the gardener taking it away. The empty tomb does not prove anything except that she has a problem. She looks and sees this figure nearby. "What's wrong," the man asked her. "Why are you crying like that?" "If you have taken him away," she replied, "just tell me and I will go get the body." And he said to her, "Mary." She looked and in his voice or manner or something about him she suddenly recognized who he was.

Now the Gospel tells us much in detail about the people in the story, but it does not tell us about Jesus' feelings at all. He is different. He no longer has fear, or indecision, or doubt. There is something about him that is strange. He is trying to teach his friends what his presence means in this world from now on. Little by little the apostles catch on. Not everyone, however, believes. Even at the very end, some of the disciples still doubt and turn away. We might ask, "Why doesn't he appear to Pilate? Why doesn't he appear to Caiphas?" Would that really have solved the problem of doubt and belief? Christ never appears to his enemies. He only appears to those who believe. He is not interested in trying to refute anybody. He is just interested in trying to get people to believe in who he is, who he was, what he is here and at this moment.

Think about the presence of Christ. Why should I be surprised, for example, if I am walking along and he suddenly appears to me? The early Church had a marvelous sense of Christ's presence. He was always there. The apostles recognized that he was different, but we never hear them talking with nostalgia about the good old days when they used to sit in the boat or when they sat on the shore of the Lake of Galilee and watched things there. They do not talk about the good old days at all. They recognized that those past events were important but they lived in the present and Christ is present with them. At the end, when Christ is about to vanish from their sight for good, he tells them, "I want you to go back to Jerusalem and I want you to pray for the coming of the Holy Spirit" (cf. Luke 24:46-53). Astonishingly, they go back rejoicing.

Now, if I were going to take a close friend to a plane and he told me: "I am never going to see you again, but I want you to go back and carry on my memory," I would go back overwhelmingly sad, feeling that he and I are separated. Yet when the apostles went back to the upper room to pray, they went back, as Scripture says, with joy. Why? Because they had a sense that Christ was present. They were not separated. I think that what we have lost today in our own Christian tradition is the vivid sense of Christ's presence. He is creating an enduring kingdom in this world. He is asking us to enter into it and to share it.

Now, when we consider all this, we look upon it in a different way than when we meditate about his breaking bread or multiplying it for the people as a past event. Christ here and now is lord of history, is master of every event in our lives. Everything that happens, e.g., your coming here tonight, interests him. Your weariness, your tiredness at the end of the day—he is interested in that. Gradually we begin to see what it means to find him in every event. He is present in every event. Of course, it is a different Christ than I thought about as I watched him along the Lake of Galilee before his death and spoke to him there. He appears only to his disciples; they form a new group and they are conscious of themselves as forming a new group which is going to carry on this tradition. Just as Abraham and his family were witnesses in the world that God is one, so this new group are witnesses that Jesus Christ came into this world. He died, he arose, and he is present in our midst.

The great truth of our religion is not simply that Christ rose from the dead, but that Christ rose from the dead and is now present! Paul is always telling us not to be discouraged, not to give up. What if the world looks as if it is on the verge of an atomic disaster! Christ has everything well in hand, he is working towards his goal and he is asking me to help him. I have to acquire that sense of being part of what he is trying to do: building the Kingdom. It is a continuing sense of sharing with him his own life. The fact that he has chosen to remain in our midst has meaning for the world. He said the same thing in the Gospels in a more general way. "Yet not a single sparrow falls to the ground without your Father's consent. As for you, every hair of your head has been counted" (Matt 10:29-30). We know all these things. As we contemplate the resurrection, he is reminding us of his presence today.

This created for the early Christians a kind of tension, too. They knew that he was present in the group that awaited the Holy Spirit. They knew that Christ was present in their celebration of the Eucharist. (Always a great Eucharistic prayer of theirs was "*Maranatha*—Lord Jesus, come!") They knew he was present when a group of them gathered together, and they thought about him and discussed him. Yet there was another sense in which he was present. They could not quite grasp it, but they would go out from the Eucharist with this sense that maybe they would run into him. I think, too, that is why so many of them thought of the *Parousia,* i.e., of the final coming. If I knew that I had a good friend in a room nearby, I might be constantly looking around expecting to see him. The early Christians had that sense that they were apt to run into Jesus, that he would suddenly appear.

The first literature of the Church is not the Gospels but St. Paul's letters, about Christ working in the Christian community. And Paul says, maybe some of you did know Christ, but that is not the way you know him now, even if you saw him in the flesh (cf. 2Co 5:16). We know him now as he actually is in our midst. It is a different sense of his presence. Until we retrieve such perception of Christ ourselves, I think we are always going to falter and fail, give up without the courage to keep trying to see what God wants us to do. The realization that the risen Christ not only directs history but is part of it, and that he is using me to help in this constant chain of historical events can give new life to my prayer.

Contemplation on Divine Love

The Contemplation to Attain the Love of God I am going to assume is part of the Fourth Week. There was much argument in past centuries about that. This contemplation begins with two suppositions [230–231]. They are ordinary suppositions from psychology that we usually take for granted. The first is simply this: that love is expressed more deeply in action than in words. We have a hundred popular songs in the English language that say much of the same thing. Many times in families people take love for granted. "I told you I loved you. Isn't that enough?" "No!" A hug is often worth a hundred words. You show people that you genuinely love them. That is important. That ordinary principle of psychology is true in relation to God. God said such splendid things in Scripture. He compares himself to a mother (cf Isa 49:15). How often he says, I have lifted you up as a mother lifts her child and holds her cheek against his. That is beautiful! God speaks about his deep friendship, how he has given his life for us. Yet when you look back on what he has done, how far and away is it better than everything he says. You know the beautiful passages in the New Testament as well. Christ compares himself to the shepherd, for example, going after the lost sheep and many other such images. Yet the marvelous things he has done for us in each of our lives, we could not possibly tell. For God, too, actions speak louder than words.

The second supposition states that when we love someone, we gradually want to share with one another little by little of what we are and possess, so that both give and receive until a kind of equality is attained. If a man, for example, is poor and a woman falls in love with him, and she has money, she wants to share it with him. A wife is sickly and the husband has strength; he wants to share his strength with her. A mother looks at her child who is lost or confused, and she knows which way to turn, so she wants to share that with him. Whenever we love somebody, we always want to share. A long time ago Cicero said that when we share pain with someone, it cuts it in half. When we share joy with someone, it doubles the joy for oneself—just being able to tell the other about it. A brother might even love his sister so much that he might want to give her a part of his candy bar. In any case this kind of sharing we all recognize. That is the way God has been.

God created us not to acquire anything. He was infinitely happy and He wanted to share that happiness. There wasn't anything or anybody to share it with so he made an image of himself. Suppose I had a great picture that gave me extraordinary pleasure and I wanted to share it with my friends. I would have copies of that picture made. I would give it to my friends so they would get the same kind of pleasure I got out of it. God also wanted to share happiness. God created us to his own image so that we could somehow or other share in that divine life. God often compares himself to a parent giving life. As a mother gives life to the child in her womb, so God gives us life. Then God wanted to give us his Son, to give us a fuller share in his life. So God shared with us his Son and the Holy Spirit. God is like a fountain that overflows.

Let us imagine that God is present. Suppose we see out into infinite space. God is around us. Give us, we ask, a sense of all the gifts God has given us so that knowing the gifts we begin to appreciate them, be blessed with them. Suddenly we will come to know that giver. Chesterton compares God to a great servant. Before we get up in the morning, God comes out and spreads the table. He sets the sunrise. He makes the trees and the flowers. Every one of those things is God's gift to us. How many sunsets have we seen for which we have forgotten to thank God? Yet all these are gifts to us.

Let us consider the great gift for each of us of our mothers. God just does not give us any mother. He gave each of us this particular one for me. She gave us life, and the life she gave us was God's gift to each of us. She gave us food. That also was his gift. Think as well of the great gift of our fathers and his work for us. His love was different from our mothers'. There was a strength about it, a tenacity about it. Yet it was God's gift to us, too, just as much as a mother's gift of love. Or we have seen teachers with the excellent imagination, skill, memory and the ability to bridge and explain things. These are all things that God gives us. These are but a reflection of God's knowledge and imagination and skills.

We ought not, however, just think about them, but count them off and write them down. Did you ever clean out a desk, open a drawer, and find there some old letters? You don't want to throw them away and you read them. You handle them fondly again. That is the way we should go through this memory of these gifts. Taste and touch them and let them come back. They are like souvenirs all the time. You take them up, and you turn them over and you think about them. Then you ask, "Who is this God that is always giving us these many things. Who is he?"

The sun tells us something of his brightness. Sometimes you sit on a bench and you feel the gentleness of a breeze and it tells you of the coolness and the healing touch of God. You look at the mountains and you see the vastness of God. How long they have been there! It seems like forever. The Grand Canyon and the other wonders of the world portray something of the color and endless variety of God. When we walk on the green grass and the grass springs up underneath our feet, it tells us something about how God's life goes on all the time. Look at a rose and see the petals. Or we see a child's ear and the delicacy of it and it tells us something about God's skill and artistry. Then we begin to wonder. Every one of these gifts tells us in some small way who God is.

Take everything in our lives, we can go through all the gifts, and God is there *working* with them, too. So God is not only present in all these gifts, He is always working with them. He is thinking as our father works and thinking along with him. He is helping our mothers to give us life. He is not only present there, but he is working with her in giving that life. As the food is growing up from the ground, he is there like a gardener taking care of it. As the trees blossom, bloom and gain strength, God is there, too. He gives strength and support to the mountains and the rocks and to the sea. In everything God is working all the time; he is restless. The sea is a reminder of the great restless activity of God. He not only gives us these gifts; he is not only present, but he is also working with us all the time.

God sent his Son into the world to show us something of the way he comes to us. Christ brought us many things. He brought us hope; he brought us faith. He brought us forgiveness of sins, but he came with those gifts, too, and he gives them to each one of us. He tries to nourish us in the Eucharist. He is trying to give us this bread which will give us life. When we pray for daily bread we are praying for food for the mind and for the heart. So Christ gives us food in the Eucharist to nourish us. We often think of the Mass as looking back. However, it is a gift for the present too, nourishing and providing us strength to live this life of Christ's presence in the world.

God sent too that wonderful woman who would be the mother of his Son and he showed us her heart and her steadfastness, her quiet care of her Son. We learned something about this quality of God, too. In Scripture he spoke much about the feminine qualities of God, but in his mother we begin to see other qualities, too, that are his.

If I loved someone very much, I could call up the May Company here in Cleveland or O'Neill's in Akron, and I would say, I want to send this girl that I love very much something special, a box of candy, or a blouse, or a handkerchief. I would order it and have it delivered to her. Or, I might love her so much that I would go down and look it over, pick it out, and bring it to her myself. That would show a greater kind of love. That is the way God gives all his gifts to us. If I got this present from the store, had it wrapped up, and I brought it to you, there is something special about it isn't there? That is the way with God's gifts. He just does not put them out there and say, "Well, you take this one or that one." He brings us every single gift himself. He not only gives us things; he comes himself with the gift.

Well, what should be our response? I said at the beginning that the great gift that we get in the *Exercises* is the gift of freedom. At the end we give this freedom back to God. As we begin to think of everything that God has given us, we begin to say: "Take Lord, receive all my liberty" [234]. You gave me my freedom, my liberty, my memory, my understanding— give me only your love and your grace, and I am rich enough and desire nothing more.

One time, on Mount Tabor, for a brief time the apostles saw Jesus, God's Son glowing in transfiguration. Something of his divinity began to break through and they could not stand it. Then a cloud came over them. Peter was so taken by the experience that he said: "Let us never go away. Let us stay here forever" (Cf. Mark 9:2-8). What would it be if someday Christ should tell us a little about who his Father is? We always have to come to the Father and to the Holy Spirit through him. If Jesus of Nazareth, present here, now, in this room, was so overwhelming for them, then what must the Father be like?

Only God can answer that question. All we can do is say, take and receive. Give me only your love and your grace, and I am rich enough and desire nothing more.

NOTES

[1]F. X. Durrwell, *The Resurrection* (New York: Sheed and Ward, 1960).

[2]David M. Stanley, *Christ's Resurrection in Pauline Soteriology* (Rome: Pontifico Instituto Biblico, 1961).

[3]Compare [299].

10

The Core Experience of the *Spiritual Exercises* and Ignatian Spirituality Today

John E. Dister, S.J.

The preceding chapters have offered us not only a good overview of what the *Spiritual Exercises* are all about, but, I suggest, some fine insights into their dynamics that have not been noted before, at least in this fashion. What I propose to attempt here is to reflect on the heart of the inspiration of the *Exercises*. I suggest that a summary of the core experience and fruit of the *Spiritual Exercises* is an apt way to conclude this series.

My remarks about the inspiration of Ignatian spirituality are threefold. First, I want to talk about Ignatius' personal *experience* of the triune God as "creator and Lord" and the consequences of this. Second, I want to discuss that character of Ignatian spirituality that involves a developing *personal encounter with Christ in the present time*. Lastly, I want to say a few things about the relation between Ignatian spirituality and service and what this might teach us about our spiritual life as Christians in general.

It is then first of all extremely important to note that the *Exercises* are the result of Inigo's own personal experience of God entering into his life consequent upon his conversion. At Loyola during his convalescence, in his encounters with the Lord at Manresa, and in the intellectual visions at the river Cardoner, Ignatius experientially encountered the Lord. Walter Farrell in chapter 3 has shown this for us clearly. Although this means that the *Exercises* result from Ignatius' own rather profound mystical experience, it does not mean that one has to be a mystic, least of all in the usual romanticized understanding of that term, in order to benefit from the *Spiritual Exercises*. Here I will not repeat the historical development of Ignatius' experience after his conversion that Walter Farrell gave us nor explain Ignatius' autobiography where we are told of these experiences.

I shall, however, simply underscore the nature of those experiences. The content of these experiences seem to have related to the majesty of God and some insights concerning the Trinity. He saw God behind the activity of all creatures. These experiences seem also to have involved insight into the humanity of Christ and his presence in the Eucharist.[1] For our purposes here, however, in understanding the nature of the *Exercises*, there are two fundamental principles of Ignatius' teaching that grew out of these early months of Ignatius' life after his conversion: First and most important, is the fact that the Christian can experience God directly in some genuine sense of these words. Karl Rahner implies that this insight is the most important contribution to the Church that Ignatius of Loyola has made.[2] The second principle is the realization that God is acting in history, our world. Although this latter is a premise to the whole Judeo-Christian religion, the point here is that Ignatius taught us that this is *experienced* in our own prayer lives.

From these two principles, which combined can be formulated as "the experience of God acting in our history," result the following consequences for Christian spirituality. First, these two principles involve specifically what classically in the context of the *Exercises* have been called the discernment of spirits and the discernment of God's will. What this means still more concretely is that by reflecting on the alternations of consolation and desolation experienced in prayer, we can come to know what God is saying to us in the particular circumstances of our lives today. Intuitively, of course, many women and men of prayer, without any help from Ignatius, know that prayer helps them to find God's will for them. What Ignatius contributed was a careful methodology, embodied in his "Rules for the Discernment of Spirits" and in the process of the election in the *Exercises*, for coming more clearly to such discernment. Jules Toner has already given us an admirable summary of this important dimension of the *Exercises* in chapter 6. There is no way in which I can here embark upon a further explanation of Ignatian discernment. I will, however, venture the following. Especially in conjunction with what we will say later concerning union with Christ in his abjectness and suffering, where there is experienced in prayer a peace that is more than the release from the necessary tension of decision-making, it is usually a clear indication that we are on the right path to the Lord. Particularly if this peace is experienced in a dynamic openness to the future, God's future, no matter what it may bring, and there is no discernible parity between the content of my prayer and the resulting experience, then it is likely from the Lord. This surely is not saying much, but at least it is more than nothing and is at the heart of Ignatian discernment.

A second consequence of Ignatius' teaching resulting from his experiences at Manresa is what it says to us concerning the activity of the Holy Spirit and the sensitivity of men and women to God's action in their lives. Whatever one may think about the recent growth of Neo-Pentecostalism and the Charismatic Movement, it has mirrored to Christian consciousness the failure adequately to account for the presence and activity of the Holy Spirit in everyday Christian life. If God is experienced directly in human life by consolation and desolation in the discernment of various spirits, it is by the gifts of the Holy Spirit that this discernment takes place. Tad Dunne in chapter 2 helped us to account for the silence of Ignatius on the Spirit in the "spirit-phobia" of his time and to demonstrate how important the activity of the Spirit was for understanding the *Exercises*. Ignatian discernment, therefore, commends and indeed demands a great sensitivity to the Holy Spirit.

A third consequence of Ignatius' insight on God's activity in our lives is the requisite detachment or indifference for responding to God's action. The well known place of this "indifference" in the *Exercises* is not that of a Stoic, nor the ideal of nirvana, but the freedom which allows us to respond to God's action. The model of Ignatian detachment is Christ in the garden, detached from his own will and submissive to the will of his Father, but hardly emotionally detached, much less stoical, in his poignant situation. In the progress of the *Spiritual Exercises,* this detachment is both held out as an ideal for the unfolding of the process of the *Exercises* and is one of the objectives of many of the Ignatian meditations and contemplations. This freedom to be moved by God has been compared to the ability of a ball bearing to be moved wherever our finger chooses to push it. Such detachment is at the core of the *Exercises*.

A final consequence of Ignatius' contribution on direct experience of God in our lives is the famous Ignatian principle of "finding God in all things." I sometimes fear that this is talked about much more than it is experienced. As a more than transitory quality of our prayer lives, it is the fruit not merely of the *Exercises* but of a continuing and deep prayer life.

The second main topic I want to discuss is that character of the *Exercises* that involves a developing *personal encounter with Christ in the present*. Now surely in some sense this is characteristic of all genuine Christian spiritualities in the Church and is not peculiar to Ignatius and the *Exercises*. Yet there is a *specific* "feel" or horizon or taste of the personal encounter with Christ in the *Exercises* that must be looked at carefully. From the outset of this section I would like to share with you the following conviction that has grown in me over the years: viz., despite the emphasis which Ignatius places on the historical life of Jesus as encountered in the Gospels, as in his contemplations on the life of Christ, and despite his silence on the Holy Spirit in the *Exercises*, and despite the fact that he nowhere in them recommends for prayer or reading the letters of Paul, I think that Ignatius' fundamental approach to Christ in the *Exercises* is Pauline. By "Pauline" I mean the sense of the recurring phrase of Paul's letters, "in Christ Jesus" or "with Christ" or in the sense of the mysticism behind the words in Galatians, "Now not I, but Christ lives in me." Another way of expressing this is to suggest that the encounter with Christ Ignatius envisages in the *Exercises* is not primarily with the *Christ of history*, of his life in the past, but with the *Christ of mystery* living and working now in his Body as well as reigning victorious with the Father. This is simply the outcome of his Manresa experiences. If this conviction is well founded (and I am not the first to have proposed it[3]) and if it had been more widely reflected upon, perhaps there would have been fewer barrels of ink exhausted in recent decades attempting to reconcile Ignatius' contemplations on the life of Christ with the outcome of biblical criticism and New Testament scholarship.

The encounter with Christ is for Ignatius, however, not just with a Lord reigning gloriously but in a hidden fashion in the Body of Christ today. It is as well with a Christ laboring and suffering even today. This is again in the context of Pauline theology which grew from the experience of Christ encountering Saul with the words, "Saul, why do you persecute me?" (AA 9:4). Moreover, it is a Christ very personally encountered as provider, as protector, as leader and as friend, in the imagery of the vassal-Lord relationship of feudal society as Kenneth Galbraith reminded us in chapter 5. Here we find all the distinctive and historically conditioned terminology of Ignatius' famous meditations on the Kingdom of Christ and the Two Standards. Galbraith showed us as well the hurdles to be surmounted here both in the sexist and in the military language which Ignatius uses. But he showed us as well the value of the language to be translated. Let us notice very carefully what we are saying here. The peculiar feel of one's personal encounter with Christ through the *Exercises* cannot be dismissed without jeopardy to a fundamental insight resulting from Ignatius' own encounter with Jesus the Lord at Manresa. Ignatius could only use the language and the mythology of the time in which he lived, a time, as both Robert Schmitt and Galbraith have pointed out, that was still redolent with late medieval ideals of courtly love, of the friendship of vassalage, and deep personal loyalties between men.

Again, the insight into our personal relationship to Christ expressed by Ignatius in feudal imagery cannot simply be dismissed, either by revisionist historian or feminist scholar, without violating one of the most important contributions Ignatius has made. Some of you may have read Patrick Arnold's recent book or article[4] attempting to show the analogous problem of maintaining genuine models of masculine spirituality while addressing the just claims of feminists against the patriarchal domination of our culture. But, of course, the sexist and otherwise inappropriate metaphors and the language of the *Exercises* can and indeed must be translated. Galbraith has provided us a beginning on how to do so. Particularly helpful perhaps was his suggestion that the very emphasis that Ignatius puts on imagination in the mediation on the Kingdom of Christ (and elsewhere) allows us to transform the historically conditioned image of king into *my ideal*, i.e., to find the divine stamp of approval on who the Lord wants me to be as *my transcendent self*. To quote Father Galbraith:

> Springing from my imagination and attracting all my energies because I myself have fashioned him as ideal, this imaginative leader is ultimately nothing more than *my transcendent self:* a reflection of everything I want to be as a full, human person. And because God would not choose as the fulfillment of the human heart a person who would not reflect all that God himself is, I can come to appreciate in a wholly new way that my transcendent self images the divine, that in moving to live out that which my imagination and heart have shown me what I am moving to become, I am reaching to the divine within me.[5]

It is beyond the scope of this presentation for me to try to do much to continue here this necessary enterprise of translation of the Ignatian metaphors. For our purposes in prayer, the issue is simply the reality pointed to by such words as the following from the *Exercises:*

> It is my will to conquer the whole world and all my enemies, and thus to enter into the glory of my Father. Therefore, whoever wishes to join me in this enterprise must be willing to labor with me, that by following me in suffering, he may follow me in glory [Kingdom of Christ, 95].

> Here it will be to ask for an intimate knowledge of our Lord, who has become man for me, that I may love Him more and follow him more closely [Second Week, First Contemplation, 104].

> [I]n order to imitate and be in reality more like Christ our Lord, I desire and choose poverty with Christ poor, rather than riches; insults with Christ loaded with them, rather than honors; I desire to be accounted as worthless and a fool for Christ, rather than to be esteemed as wise and prudent in this world. So Christ was treated before me [Three Kinds of Humility, 167].

The fierce dedication to and love for the person of Christ, the allowing oneself through self-offering to be bound to him in fealty and shared labor, in suffering and joy, such as are expressed in these passages and in the meditations and contemplations from which they come, are clearly at the heart of the *Exercises* and, accordingly, of the inspiration of Ignatius and his contribution to the Church.

What then seems to follow from all this for our day-to-day Christian lives? Two things come particularly to mind: the genuine nature of the imitation of Christ and a deepening understanding of what we today often call the "paschal mystery." First, the following of Christ in the *Exercises* is not *mimicry* of the life of Jesus of Nazareth. It is allowing the uniqueness of our own individual personalities to develop under the guidance of the grace of Christ, according to the pattern revealed by his life in the Scriptures. There may be a genuine place in the spiritualities of the Church for mimicking the details of Jesus' life, as has been suggested is more easily related to the Franciscan tradition, but it is not what Ignatius is trying to get us to see and do. I think again that a Pauline understanding of our life in Christ is implied here.

Second, the *Exercises* lead us deeply into what since the liturgical renewal and Vatican II we have frequently called "the paschal mystery," i.e., our sharing in the death and resurrection of Jesus. This is more than just reminding ourselves that in the third and fourth weeks of the *Exercises* we spend a great deal of time contemplating Jesus in his passion and risen life. It means, again in the context of Pauline mysticism, that Christ is laboring and suffering, and is humble and poor *today,* not just that he was so in his historical life two thousand years ago. But it also means that we share *today* in Jesus' joy, and glory, and consolation, and that this is not just something that we wait for on that day when we shall share with Jesus his glory with the Father.

The final main topic I want to discuss on Ignatian spirituality has to do with the notion of service. The first insight that grows out of the *Exercises* was how God is experienced as acting directly in our lives. The second one was that God acts through our developing encounter with Jesus the Christ acting and living in us today. Now these together also imply that we who are laboring and suffering with and in Christ today and who share in his glory are *serving* God. Our personal relation to Christ, our Lord acting in history, *is* service of God in his Church.

This is a fundamental premise of the *Exercises* with at least two important implications: First, they do not lead to an individualistic spirituality, despite the non-communal or individualistic character of the prayer itself. The locale of the enterprise of laboring lovingly with Christ is always social. It is the human family and the Church (more specifically, I should perhaps use the classical terminology of the Church "militant"). Second, this service involves battle, battle with the power of darkness, of evil in history and in our personal lives. No matter what one's personal theological stance may be on the existence of personal demons and devils, or of

Satan that Ignatius calls, interestingly, "the enemy of human nature," for him there can be no doubt of the battle with the powers of evil, whether they lie in the hearts of women and men or even in some cosmic forces of Pauline principalities and powers.

Another important aspect of the notion of service is, of course, the Ignatian preoccupation with the "glory of God." This gaining for God, or giving to Him what is already His, is simply identical with what Ignatius otherwise calls "the good of souls" (i.e., apostolic zeal). This follows necessarily, I again suggest, from the insight of Christ actively present in our history.

Now a final word on what seems to follow from all this for the nature of prayer in the mind of Ignatius, whether or not making the *Spiritual Exercises* of St. Ignatius is something for us. Clearly, as I have suggested, Ignatius has contributed to the tradition of prayer within the Church the fundamental insights that (1) we can experience God acting directly in our lives; (2) that this happens in a most poignant fashion with a developing encounter with Christ living and working with us in our personal histories; and (3) that our response to the combination of these two constitute the service of God and the Church. And this service in turn involves a struggle for the good of souls and for God's greater glory, which all mean the same thing for Ignatius. There has been brewing for many decades a dispute among commentators on the *Spiritual Exercises* as to whether they are primarily a process of decision making for the apostolically zealous Church person or a "school of prayer," particularly of contemplative prayer. The battle was drawn in most recent times, at least in the mind of one of the antagonists, between Fr. William Peters on the contemplation side and the Rahner brothers, Hugo and Karl, on the side of the "election," as it has been called, or Christian decision-making.[6] Who is correct? The answer, I suggest, is "Yes." The *Exercises* are simultaneously, on the one hand, active and decisive; they embrace reason, method, order, discipline and "meditation" in the classical use of that word. But, on the other hand, they are also passive and encompass the emotions, affectivity, and "contemplation" in the classical sense of that word.

Ignatius through his *Exercises* has anticipated the growing conviction of our times that mysticism and the contemplative life do not constitute an esoteric claim of a chosen few, a romanticized life of an elect, a kind of neo-Gnosticism, but rather a dimension of Christian life generally. (In passing, let me say that it should be obvious that by "mysticism" and contemplative prayer I am not referring to unusual phenomena such as imaginative visions, ecstasy, levitation, etc. About these Ignatius, like St. John of the Cross, had very great suspicions.) Ignatius' outlook was that intimate contact with Christ and the experience of God in prayer is at the heart of the apostolic life. Joseph de Guibert has rightly called Ignatius' mysticism a mysticism of service in contrast with a mysticism of union.[7] This is something that should be remembered when, again in our current times of deepening interest in mysticism and prayer, there might be the tendency to use contemplation as an escape from the many social problems and crises of justice which plague us. Such an escapist attitude can in no wise be reconciled with Ignatius and the *Exercises*. He adamantly opposed some of his colleagues who tried to transform some Jesuit houses into quasi-contemplative communities. He had definite reservations about lengthy prayer.[8] Perhaps this is not totally applicable to our manifestly different cultural situation. But this attitude from so great a mystic himself, so fiercely devoted to Christ his Lord, still tells us today, in any event, about the necessary relationship between Ignatian spirituality and action.

NOTES

[1]Cf. A 28–30 and Walter L. Farrell, ch. 3, passim.

[2]See Karl Rahner, *Ignatius of Loyola,* with an Historical Introduction by Paul Imhoff, S.J., tr. Rosaleen Ockenden (London: Collins, 1979) 11–15. Cf. also Rahner's, *The Dynamic Element in the Church* (New York: Seabury, 1964) 84ff.

[3]See Hugo Rahner, *Ignatius the Theologian* (New York: Herder and Herder, 1968) 96–100 and commentators generally on Ignatius' view of Christ as "a living king actively at work here and now in this world" as in P. de Leturia, *Estudios Ignacianos,* II, Rome, 1957, 14f. cited by Rahner on 97. See also above Walter L. Farrell, ch. 3., pp. 34–35.

[4]Patrick M. Arnold, "In Search of the Hero: Masculine Spirituality and Liberal Christianity," *America,* October 7, 1989 (161) 206ff, and *Wildmen, Warriors, and Kings: Masculine Spirituality and the Bible* (New York: Crossroads, 1991).

[5]Cf. above ch. 5, p. 56.

[6]See William A. M. Peters, *The Spiritual Exercises of St. Ignatius: Exposition and Interpretation* (Rome, C. I. S., 1968), especially his treatment of the "election," 120–129. The Rahner brothers and others, as proponents of the interpretation of the Exercises that he is opposing, are not mentioned for their views on the election in this book, as they were in the many seminars he presented in the years before it was published (such as the one this author attended in Cleveland in the fall 1963). But see his Preface, xiv.

[7]Joseph de Guibert, S.J., *The Jesuits: Their Spiritual Doctrine and Practice,* tr. William J. Young, S.J., (Chicago: Loyola University Press, 1964) 178ff. Cf. also the conclusion of ch. 3, p. 39.

[8]See references in Frank J. Houdek, S.J., "Jesuit Prayer and Jesuit Ministry: Context and Possibilities," *Studies in the Spirituality of Jesuits,* 24/1 (January 1992) 3–6.